OUR CHANGING CONSTITUTION

BY

CHARLES W. PIERSON

GARDEN CITY NEW YORK
DOUBLEDAY, PAGE & COMPANY

1922

Forgotten Phoenix Press

2010

Editor's Note

Those who do not know history are doomed to repeat it. Knowing our history allows us to learn from the mistakes of the past rather than needlessly repeating blunders and disasters. But what if the history we have learned is flawed? What if we have been decieved and lied to about our history? If we do not understand and learn from that which REALLY happened, we are still doomed to relive it. We can only avoid this trap by knowing and learning from the truth, pleasant or unpleasant, and taking active steps to avoid the same disastrous pitfalls.

The past is written in stone. Unfortunately, even stone does not last forever. It erodes with time if not protected from the elements. Our past and our history have been erroded by time and human elements. History is constantly being rewritten to support the populist views of the day. Mistakes of the past are often scrubbed out and left to be forgotten, or retold and distorted to hide the truth, often under the guise of good will and political correctness. Some elements of history are painful, and we must be brave enough to deal with the pain and grow from these mistakes. Anything less is simply putting a band-aid on a broken leg and hoping it will heal. With each passing generation the level of distortion and ommissions grows greater, leaving the people ignorant and vulnerable to the repetition of the greatest failures.

The future, however, is written in sand. What appears clear today has yet to be proven by the tides of time. The words are there, waiting. Only time will tell if they will set long enough turn to stone and become part of history itself, or if they will all be washed away by the waves of the next revolution.

It is the mission of the Forgotten Phoenix to revive our history and re-educate our people, all people. We do not hide from the past, good or bad. We will not distort the events that occurred. We seek to revive the realities of the past in the context in which they occurred. The best recorders of history are those who were there, back when it was not yet history, but the current events of the day. Only in that correct context can it be correctly judged. Technology may change, but human nature forever remains the same. Most of which is occurring in the world today is not novel and new, but a repitition of history. We are reliving the mistakes our ancestors have already lived through. Now is the time to learn the truth, to learn from them what steps we need to take now, so that we may move forward and create a grand new future for the next generation to learn from.

It is knowledge that will awaken the sleeping giant, the great American Spirit, which will rise anew from the ashes of the old world. It will rise up like the mighty phoenix, because America, like Rome long ago, is burning.

Forgotten Phoenix Press

PREFACE

Citizens of the United States are wont to think of their form of government, a political system based on a written constitution, as something fixed and stable. In reality, it is undergoing a profound change. The idea which constituted its most distinctive feature, and in the belief of many represents America's most valuable contribution to the science of government, is being forgotten. Formed to be "an indestructible Union composed of indestructible states," our dual system is losing its duality. The states are fading out of the picture. The aim of this volume is to point out the change and discuss some of its aspects. A few chapters have already appeared in print. "Our Changing Constitution" and "Is the Federal Corporation Tax Constitutional?" were published in the *Outlook*. "The Corporation Tax Decision" appeared in the *Yale Law Journal*. "Can Congress Tax the Income from State and Municipal Bonds?" was printed in the *New York Evening Post*. All of these have been more or less revised and some new matter has been added.

CONTENTS

I. THE SALIENT FEATURE OF THE CONSTITUTION...7

- The American Constitution, its origin and contents. Wherein its novelty and greatness lay.
- Importance of maintaining the equilibrium established between national and state power.
- View of John Fiske.

II. THE SUPREME COURT OF THE UNITED STATES...12

- Place of the Court in the constitutional scheme.
- Its most important function.
- Personnel of the Court.
- Its power moral rather than physical. Its chief weapon the power to declare legislative acts unconstitutional.
- Limitations on this power--political questions; necessity of an actual controversy; abuses of legislative power.
- Erroneous popular impressions. Impairment of the constitutional conscience.

III. OUR CHANGING CONSTITUTION...18

- Change in popular attitude toward the Constitution.
- Causes of the change (growth of national consciousness, wars, foreign relations, influence of later immigrants and their descendants, desire to obtain federal appropriations, economic development, railroads, free trade among the states).
- Methods by which change has been put into effect (constitutional amendment, treaties, federal legislation under cover of power to regulate commerce and lay taxes).
- Attitude of the Supreme Court.
- Differences of opinion in the Court.

IV. THE EIGHTEENTH OR PROHIBITION AMENDMENT....................................28

- History and radical character of amendment.
- Efforts to defeat it in the courts.
- Unusual course taken by Supreme Court.
- Discussion of its true place in the development of American constitutional law. Less a point of departure than a spectacular manifestation of a change already under way.
- Effect of the change on the principle of local self-government.

V. THE NINETEENTH OR WOMAN SUFFRAGE AMENDMENT 36

- Attitude of the Constitution toward question of suffrage qualifications.
- Effect of Civil War amendments.
- Growth of woman suffrage movement and adoption of Suffrage Amendment. How far the amendment constitutes a federal encroachment on state power.
- Effect of woman suffrage on questions of governmental theory.

VI. CONGRESS VERSUS THE SUPREME COURT--THE CHILD LABOR LAWS.. 43

- The child labor question. Philanthropic and commercial aspects.
- Attempt of Congress to legislate under power to regulate commerce.
- Decision of Supreme Court holding law unconstitutional. The decision explained.
- Reenactment of law by Congress under cover of power to lay taxes.
- Arguments for and against constitutionality of new enactment.

VII. STATE RIGHTS AND THE SUPREME COURT...49

- The Supreme Court at first a bulwark of national power; to-day the defender of the states.
- Explanation of this apparent change.
- Attitude of the Court in the first period.
- The period of Chief Justice Marshall.

- The period of Chief Justice Taney.
- The Reconstruction Period.
- Attitude of the Court to-day.
- Reasons why the Court is unable to prevent federal encroachment.
- Attitude of Hamilton and Marshall toward state rights misunderstood.

VIII. THE FEDERAL TAXING POWER AND THE INCOME TAX AMENDMENT...59

- America's embarrassing position if the late war had come before adoption of Income Tax Amendment. Limitations of federal taxing power under the Constitution.
- Meaning of "uniformity."
- Apportionment of "direct taxes."
- The Supreme Court decision in the Income Tax cases in 1894 a reversal of long settled ideas.
- The Income Tax Amendment an example of recall of judicial decisions.
- Implied limitations on federal taxing power (compensation of federal judges, due process clause of the Constitution, no power to tax property or governmental activities of the states).

IX. CAN CONGRESS TAX THE INCOME FROM STATE AND MUNICIPAL BONDS?...66

- No express prohibition of such taxation; it lies in an implied limitation inherent in our dual system of government.
- Discussion of doctrine and its development by the Supreme Court.
- Effect of the Income Tax Amendment.
- Present dissatisfaction with doctrine and efforts to abolish it.

X. IS THE FEDERAL CORPORATION TAX CONSTITUTIONAL?.........................73

- Nature of the tax. An interference with state power to grant corporate franchises.
- Nature of our dual government and Supreme Court decisions on the subject discussed.

- The debate in Congress.

XI. THE CORPORATION TAX DECISION..82

- Importance of the decision likely to be overlooked.
- Criticism of the Court's arguments.
- Effects of the decision.

XII. THE FEDERAL GOVERNMENT AND THE TRUSTS.....................................87

- Origin and history of Sherman Act. Its meaning now clear. Earlier uncertainties owing chiefly to two questions--What is interstate trade and Does the act enlarge the common-law rule as to what restraints were unlawful?
- How these questions have been settled.
- Statement of the common-law rule. Incompatibility between the law and present economic conditions. Suggestions for legal reform. The holding company device, its abuses and the possibility of abolishing it. Advantages of the scheme of federal incorporation.

XIII. WHAT OF THE FUTURE?...95

- Rapid progress and present extent of federal encroachment on state power.
- Growth of federal bureaucracy.
- A reaction against centralization inevitable sooner or later.
- Adequacy of Constitution to deal with changing conditions.
- The railroads and the trusts. Dangerous assaults upon Constitution in field of social welfare legislation. Exercise of police power a matter for local authority.
- Elihu Root's view. Outlook for the future.

APPENDIX..100

Chapter I
THE SALIENT FEATURE OF THE CONSTITUTION

Few documents known to history have received as much praise as the United States Constitution. Gladstone called it "the most wonderful work ever struck off at a given time by the brain and purpose of man." The casual reader of the Constitution will be at a loss to account for such adulation. It will seem to him a businesslike document, outlining a scheme of government in terse and well-chosen phrases, but he is apt to look in vain for any earmarks of special inspiration. To understand the true greatness of the instrument something more is required than a mere reading of its provisions.

The Constitution was the work of a convention of delegates from the states, who met in Philadelphia in May, 1787, and labored together for nearly four months. They included a large part of the best character and intellect of the country. George Washington presided over their deliberations. The delegates had not been called together for the purpose of organizing a new government. Their instructions were limited to revising and proposing improvements in the Articles of the existing Confederation, whose inefficiency and weakness, now that the cohesive power of common danger in the war of the Revolution was gone, had become a byword. This task, however, was decided to be hopeless, and with great boldness the convention proceeded to disregard instructions and prepare a wholly new Constitution constructed on a plan radically different from that of the Articles of Confederation.

The contents of the Constitution, as finally drafted and submitted for ratification, may be described in few words. It created a legislative department consisting of a Senate and a House of Representatives, an executive department headed by a President, and a judicial department headed by a Supreme Court, and prescribed in general terms the qualifications, powers, and functions of each. It provided for the admission of new states into the Union and that the United States should guarantee to every state a republican form of government. It declared that the Constitution and the laws of the United States made in pursuance thereof, and treaties, should be the supreme law of the land. It provided a method for its own amendment. Save for a few other brief clauses, that was all. There was no proclamation of Democracy; no trumpet blast about the rights of man such as had sounded in the Declaration of Independence. On the contrary, the instrument expressly recognized human slavery, though in discreet and euphemistic phrases.

Wherein, then, did the novelty and greatness of the Constitution lie? Its novelty lay in the duality of the form of government which it created--a nation dealing directly with its citizens and yet composed of sovereign states--and in its system of checks and balances. The world had seen confederations of states. It was familiar with nations subdivided into provinces or other administrative units. It had known experiments in pure democracy. The constitutional scheme was none of these. It was something new, and its novel features were relied upon as a protection from the evils which had developed under the other plans. The greatness of the Constitution lay in its nice adjustment of the powers of government, notably the division of powers which it affected between the National Government and the states. The powers conferred on the National Government were clearly set forth. All were of a strictly national character. They covered the field of foreign relations, interstate and foreign commerce, fiscal and monetary system, post office and post roads, patents and copyrights, and jurisdiction over certain specified crimes. All other powers were reserved to the states or the people. In other words, the theory was (to quote Bryce's "The American Commonwealth") "local government for local affairs; general government for general affairs only."

The Constitution as it left the hands of its framers was not entirely satisfactory to anybody. Owing to the discordant interests and mutual jealousies of the states, it was of necessity an instrument of many compromises. One of the great compromises was that by which the small states were given as many senators as the large. Another is embalmed in the provisions recognizing slavery and permitting slaves to count in the apportionment of representatives. (The number of a state's representatives was to be determined "by adding to the whole number of free persons ... three-fifths of all other persons.") Another was the provision that direct taxes should be apportioned among the states according to population. With all its compromises, however, the Constitution embodied a great governmental principle, full of hope for the future of the country, and the state conventions to which it was submitted for ratification were wise enough to accept what was offered. Ratification by certain of the states was facilitated by the publication of that remarkable series of papers afterward known as the "Federalist." These were the work of Alexander Hamilton, James Madison, and John Jay, and first appeared in New York newspapers.

One of the objections to the new Constitution in the minds of many people was the absence of a "bill of rights" containing those provisions for the protection of individual liberty and property (e.g., trial by jury, freedom of speech, protection from unreasonable searches and seizures) which had come down from the early charters of English liberties. In deference to this sentiment a series of ten brief amendments were proposed and speedily ratified. Another amendment (No. XI) was soon afterward adopted for the purpose of doing away with the effect of a Supreme Court decision. Thereafter, save for a change in the manner of electing the President and Vice-president, the Constitution was not again amended until after the close of the Civil War, when Amendments XIII, XIV, and XV, having for their primary object the protection of the newly enfranchised Negroes, were adopted. The Constitution was not again amended until the last decade, when the Income Tax Amendment, the amendment providing for the election of Senators by popular vote, the Prohibition Amendment, and the Woman Suffrage Amendment were adopted in rapid succession. Some of these will be discussed in later chapters.

It is interesting to note that two of the amendments (No. XI, designed to prevent suits against a state without its permission by citizens of another state, and No. XVI, paving the way for the Income Tax) were called forth by unpopular decisions of the Supreme Court, and virtually amounted to a recall of those decisions by the people. These instances demonstrate the possibility of a recall of judicial decisions by constitutional methods, and tend to refute impatient reformers who preach the necessity of a more summary procedure. Such questions, however, lie outside the scope of this book. We emphasize here the fact that the great achievement of the Constitution was the creation of a dual system of government and the apportionment of its powers. That was what made it *"one of the longest reaches of constructive statesmanship ever known in the world."*[1] It offered the most promising

---

[1] Fiske: "The Critical Period of American History," p. 301.

solution yet devised for the problem of building a nation without tearing down local self-government. John Fiske, the historian, writing of the importance of preserving the constitutional equilibrium between nation and states, said:[2]

> "If the day should ever arrive (which God forbid!) when the people of the different parts of our country shall allow their local affairs to be administered by prefects sent from Washington, and when the self-government of the states shall have been so far lost as that of the departments of France, or even so far as that of the counties of England--on that day the progressive political career of the American people will have come to an end, and the hopes that have been built upon it for the future happiness and prosperity of mankind will be wrecked forever. "

If allowance be made for certain extravagances of statement, these words will serve as a fitting introduction to the discussions which follow.

---

[2] Ibid., p. 238.

John Fiske, 1878

John Fiske was born Edmund Fiske Green at Hartford, Connecticut, March 30, 1842. He was the only child of Edmund Brewster Green, of Smyrna, Delaware, and Mary Fiske Bound, of Middletown, Connecticut. His father was editor of newspapers in Hartford, New York City, and Panama, where his father died in 1852, and his widow married Edwin W. Stoughton, of New York, in 1855. On the second marriage of his mother, Edmund Fiske Green assumed the name of his maternal great-grandfather, John Fiske

As a child, Fiske exhibited remarkable precocity. He lived at Middletown during childhood, until he entered Harvard. He graduated from Harvard College in 1863 and from Harvard Law School in 1865. He had already admitted to the Suffolk bar in 1864, but never practised law. His career as author began in 1861, with an article on "Mr. Buckle's Fallacies" published in the National Quarterly Review. After that, he was a frequent contributor to American and British periodicals.

From 1869 to 1871, he was university lecturer on philosophy at Harvard, in 1870 instructor in history there, and assistant librarian 1872-1879. On resigning the latter position in 1879, he was elected a member of the board of overseers, and at the expiration of the six-year term was re-elected in 1885. Beginning in 1881, he lectured annually on American history at Washington University, St. Louis, Missouri, and beginning in 1884 held a professorship of American history at that institution, but continued to make his home in Cambridge, Massachusetts. He lectured on American history at University College London in 1879 and at the Royal Institution of Great Britain in 1880.

Chapter II
THE SUPREME COURT OF THE UNITED STATES

The Constitution effected an apportionment of the powers of government between nation and states. The maintenance of the equilibrium thus established was especially committed to the Supreme Court. This novel office, the most important of all its great functions, makes the Court one of the most vital factors of the entire governmental scheme and gives it a unique preeminence among the judicial tribunals of the world.

How the office has been performed, and whether the constitutional equilibrium is actually being maintained, are the questions to be considered in this book. Before taking them up, however, it will be useful to glance briefly at the Court itself and inquire how it is equipped for its difficult task.

The United States Supreme Court at present is composed of nine judges. The number originally was six. It now holds its sessions at the Capitol in Washington, in the old Senate Chamber which once echoed with the eloquence of the Webster-Hayne debate. The judges are nominated by the President, and their appointment, like that of ambassadors, must be confirmed by the Senate. The makers of the Constitution took the utmost care to insure the independence of the Court. Its members hold office during good behavior, that is to say for life. They cannot be removed except by impeachment for misconduct. Only one attempt has ever been made to impeach a judge of the Supreme Court[3] and that attempt failed. Still further to insure their freedom from legislative control, the Constitution provides that the compensation of the judges shall not be diminished during their continuance in office.[4]

---

[3] Justice Samuel Chase of Maryland in 1804-5.

[4] It is interesting to observe that this Court, safeguarded against popular clamor and composed of judges appointed for life, has consistently shown itself more progressive and more responsive to modern ideas than have most of the state Supreme Courts whose members are elected directly by the people and for limited terms only.

From the time of John Jay, the first Chief Justice, down to the present day the men appointed to membership in the Court have, for the most part, been lawyers of the highest character and standing, many of whom had already won distinction in other branches of the public service. The present Chief Justice (Taft) is an ex-President of the United States. Among the other members of the Court are a former Secretary of State of the United States (Justice Day); two former Attorneys General of the United States (Justices McKenna and McReynolds); a former Chief Justice of Massachusetts (Justice Oliver Wendell Holmes, the distinguished son and namesake of an illustrious father); a former Chief Justice of Wyoming (Justice Van Devanter); and a former Chancellor of New Jersey (Justice Pitney).

It is well that the personnel of the Court has been such as to command respect and deference, for in actual power the judiciary is by far the weakest of the three cooerdinate departments (legislative, executive, judicial) among which the functions of government were distributed by the Constitution. The power of the purse is vested in Congress: it alone can levy taxes and make appropriations. The Executive is Commander-in-Chief of the Army and Navy and wields the appointing power. The Supreme Court controls neither purse nor sword nor appointments to office. Its power is moral rather than physical. It has no adequate means of enforcing its decrees without the cooeperation of other branches of the Government.

That cooeperation has not always been forthcoming. In the year 1802, Congress, at the instigation of President Jefferson, the inveterate enemy of Chief Justice Marshall, suspended the sessions of the Court for more than a year by abolishing the August term. In 1832, when the State of Georgia defied the decree of the Court in a case involving the status of the Cherokee Indians, the other departments of the Federal Government gave no aid and President Andrew Jackson is reported to have remarked: "John Marshall has made the decision, now let him execute it." In 1868, Congress, in order to forestall decision in a case pending before the Court, hastily repealed the statute on which the jurisdiction of the Court depended.[5] Such instances, however, have been rare. The law-abiding instinct is strong in the American people, and for the most part the decisions of the Supreme Court have been received with respect and unquestioning obedience.

---

[5] See *ex parte McCardle*, 6 Wall. (Supreme Court Reports), 318; 7 Ibid, 506.

The chief weapon in the arsenal of the Court is the power to declare legislative acts void on the ground that they overstep limits established by the people in the Constitution. This power has been frequently exercised. It is stated that the congressional statutes thus nullified have not numbered more than thirty, while at least a thousand state laws have been nullified.[6]

The assumption of this power in the Court to declare statutes unconstitutional has been bitterly assailed, and is still denounced in some quarters, as judicial usurpation originated by John Marshall. On the historical side this objection is not well founded. Various state courts had exercised the power to declare statutes unconstitutional before the Supreme Court came into existence.[7] The framers of the Constitution clearly intended that such a power should be exercised by the Supreme Court.[8] Moreover, a somewhat similar power appears to have been exercised long before in England[9], though it gave place later to the present doctrine of the legal omnipotence of Parliament.

On the side of reason and logic, the argument in favor of the power formulated more than a century ago by Chief Justice Marshall has never been adequately answered and is generally accepted as final. He said[10]:

> "The powers of the legislature are defined and limited; and that those limits may not be mistaken or forgotten, the Constitution is written. To what purpose are powers limited, and to what purpose is that limitation committed to writing, if these limits may, at any time, be passed by those intended to be restrained?... The Constitution is either a superior paramount law, unchangeable by ordinary means, or it is on a level with ordinary legislative acts, and, like other acts, is alterable when the legislature shall please to alter it. If the former part of the alternative be true, then a legislative act, contrary to the Constitution, is not law: if the latter part be true, then written

---

[6] Brief of Solicitor General James M. Beck in the Child Labor Tax cases. It is to be borne in mind that there are forty-eight state legislatures and only one Congress.

[7] See Bryce: "The American Commonwealth," Vol. I, p. 250.

[8] See e.g., "Federalist," No. LXXVIII

[9] See opinion of Lord Coke in Bonham's Case, 8 Coke's Reports, 118, decided in 1610.

[10] *Marbury v. Madison*, 1 Cranch, 176.

constitutions are absurd attempts, on the part of the people, to limit a power in its own nature illimitable."

It would seem at first blush that the power in the Court to declare legislative acts unconstitutional affords a complete safeguard against congressional encroachment on the prerogatives of the states. Such is not the fact, however. The veto power of the Court by no means covers the entire field of legislative activity. In the Convention which framed the Constitution, attempts were made to give to the judiciary, in conjunction with the executive, complete power of revision over legislative acts, but all such propositions were voted down[11]. As matters stand, there may be violations of the Constitution by Congress (or for that matter by the executive) of which the Court can take no cognizance.

For one thing, the Court cannot deal with questions of a political character. The function of the Court is judicial only. Upon this ground it was decided that the question which of two rival governments in the State of Rhode Island was the legitimate one was for the determination of the political department of government rather than the courts;[12] that the question, whether the adoption by a state of the initiative and referendum violated the provision of the Federal Constitution guaranteeing to every state a republican form of government, was political and therefore beyond the jurisdiction of the Court.[13] In 1867 a sovereign state sought to enjoin the President of the United States from enforcing an act of Congress alleged to be unconstitutional. The Supreme Court, without determining the constitutionality of the act, declined to interfere with the exercise of the President's political discretion.[14] In the famous Dred Scott case,[15] the effort of the Supreme Court to settle a political question accomplished nothing, save to impair the influence and prestige of the Court.

The power of the Court to declare legislative acts unconstitutional is subject to another important limitation. The judicial power is limited by the

---

[11] See e.g., Farrand: "Records of the Federal Convention," Vol. I, pp. 138 et seq.; Vol. II, p. 298.

[12] Luther v. Borden 7 Howard, 1.

[13] Pacific Telephone Co. v. Oregon , 223 U.S., 118.

[14] State of Mississippi v. Andrew Johnson, 4 Wall., 475.

[15] Dred Scott v. Sandford, 19 Howard, 393.

Constitution to actual cases and controversies between opposing parties. The Court cannot decide moot questions or act as an adviser for other departments of the government. A striking illustration is found in the so-called Muskrat case.[16] Congress having legislated concerning the distribution of property of the Cherokee Indians, and doubts having arisen as to the constitutional validity of the legislation, Congress passed another act empowering one David Muskrat and other Cherokee citizens to file suit, naming the United States as defendant, to settle the question. The Supreme Court declined to take jurisdiction and dismissed the suit, holding that it was not a case or controversy between opposing parties within the meaning of the Constitution.

Still another limitation is encountered in cases involving abuse of legislative power rather than lack of power. If Congress passes an act within one of the powers expressly conferred upon it by the Constitution, for example the power to lay taxes or the power to regulate interstate commerce, the Supreme Court cannot interfere though the incidental effect and ulterior purpose of the legislation may be to intrude upon the field of state power. We shall have occasion to refer to this limitation more than once in later chapters.

An impression is abroad that the Supreme Court has plenary power to preserve the Constitution. Hence the tendency of groups to demand, and of legislators to enact, any kind of a law without regard to its constitutional aspect, leaving that to be taken care of by the Court. Any such impression is erroneous and unfortunate. It puts upon the Court a burden beyond its real powers. It undermines the sense of responsibility which should exist among the elected representatives of the people. It impairs what someone has called the constitutional conscience, and weakens the vigilance of the people in preserving their liberties. Men and women need to be reminded that the duty of upholding the Constitution does not devolve upon the Supreme Court alone. It rests upon all departments of government and, in the last analysis, upon the people themselves.

---

[16] Muskrat v. United States, 219 U.S., 346.

Dred Scott

Dred Scott v. Sandford, 60 U.S. (19 How.) 393 (1857), commonly referred to as The Dred Scott Decision, was a decision by the United States Supreme Court that ruled that people of African descent imported into the United States and held as slaves, or their descendants[2]—whether or not they were slaves—were not protected by the Constitution and could never be citizens of the United States.[3] It also held that the United States Congress had no authority to prohibit slavery in federal territories. The Court also ruled that because slaves were not citizens, they could not sue in court. Lastly, the Court ruled that slaves—as chattel or private property—could not be taken away from their owners without due process. The Supreme Court's decision was written by Chief Justice Roger B. Taney.

Although Dred Scott was never overruled by the Supreme Court itself, in the Slaughter-House Cases of 1873 the Court stated that at least one part of it had already been overruled in 1868 by the Fourteenth Amendment.

While the name of the case is "Scott vs. Sandford", the respondent's surname was actually "Sanford". A clerk misspelled the name, and the court never corrected the error. Vishneski, John (1988). "What the Court Decided in Dred Scott v. Sandford".

Chapter III
OUR CHANGING CONSTITUTION

In a celebrated case[17] decided a few years ago the Supreme Court of the United States said:

> "The Constitution is a written instrument. As such its meaning does not alter. That which it meant when adopted it means now. Being a grant of powers to a government its language is general, and as changes come in social and political life it embraces in its grasp all new conditions which are within the scope of the powers in terms conferred. In other words, while the powers granted do not change, they apply from generation to generation to all things to which they are in their nature applicable. This in no manner abridges the fact of its changeless nature and meaning. Those things which are within its grants of power, as those grants were understood when made, are still within them, and those things not within them remain still excluded....
>
> To determine the extent of the grants of power we must, therefore, place ourselves in the position of the men who framed and adopted the Constitution, and inquire what they must have understood to be the meaning and scope of those grants."

Thus speaks the voice whose word is law.

Viewed in the sense intended--as the formulation of a legal rule for the interpretation and construction of a written instrument--the statement compels assent. As a statement of historical and political fact, however, it would not be accepted so readily. An acute critic of our institutions has said that the Constitution "has changed in the spirit with which men regard it, and therefore in its own spirit."[18] Men realize that the words of the Constitution, like the words of Holy Writ, have not always meant the same thing to those

---

[17] South Carolina v. United States, 199 U.S., 437.
[18] Bryce: "The American Commonwealth," Vol. I, p. 400.

who regulate their conduct by its precepts; that the system of government which those words embody has in reality changed, is changing to-day.

The makers of the Constitution represented the people of distinct and independent states, jealous of their rights and of each other but nevertheless impelled by experience of danger lately past and sense of other perils impending to substitute for their loose and ill-working confederation a more effective union. The most formidable obstacle, apart from mutual jealousies, was a fear of loss of liberties, state and individual, through encroachment of the central power. The instrument, drawn with this fear uppermost, was designed to limit the National Government to "the irreducible minimum of functions absolutely needed for the national welfare."[19] To this end the powers granted were specifically enumerated. All other powers were by express enactment[20] "reserved to the States respectively, or to the people."

The strength of the popular sentiment against any encroachment of federal power was speedily demonstrated in a striking and dramatic way. Under the grant of power to determine controversies "between a state and citizens of another state"[21] the Supreme Court in 1793 proceeded to entertain a suit by one Chisholm, a citizen of South Carolina, against the State of Georgia.[22] It had not been supposed that the grant of power contemplated such a suit against a state without its consent. The decision aroused an indescribable state of popular fury, not only in Georgia but throughout the Union, and led to the adoption of a constitutional amendment[23] prohibiting such suits in future.

There is a long step between such an attitude toward the Constitution and the viewpoint which finds in it authority for the enactment by Congress of White Slave and Child Labor laws. Obviously there has been a profound change in what the Constitution means to its adherents. It will be

---

[19] Bryce, "The American Commonwealth," Vol. I, p. 324.

[20] Tenth Amendment

[21] Art. III, Sec. 2.

[22] See 2 Dallas, 419

[23] Eleventh Amendment

interesting to consider briefly what has caused the change of view, and how it has been put into effect.

To one searching for causes the most striking phenomenon is the growth of a national consciousness. At the outset it was practically non-existent. To-day its power has astonished enemy and friend alike. Its growth has been due to both pressure from without and developments within. Our foreign wars, especially the war with Germany, have drawn the people together and enhanced the importance of interests purely national. Some of our other foreign relations have brought into relief the advantages of a strong central government as well as certain inconveniences of our system as it left the hands of the framers. Witness the embarrassment toward Italy growing out of lack of federal jurisdiction in respect of the New Orleans riots, and the ever-present danger to our relations with Japan from acts of the sovereign State of California which the Federal Government is powerless to control. Among developments from within was the Civil War, with its triumph for the idea of national supremacy and an indissoluble union. Another, which has hardly received the attention it deserves, has been the influence of the large element of our population composed of immigrants since the Revolution and their descendants. The state sovereignty doctrine was not a mere political dogma but had its roots in history. It was an expression of the pride of the inhabitants of the Thirteen Colonies in their respective commonwealths. To them it stood for patriotism and traditions. These feelings the later immigrant neither shared nor understood. When he gave up his Old World allegiance and emigrated he came to America, not to New York or Massachusetts. To him the nation was everything, the state merely an administrative subdivision of the nation.

Another cause has been the desire to obtain aid in local matters from the national treasury. This has proved an exceedingly potent and insidious influence, leading state officials to surrender voluntarily state prerogatives in exchange for appropriations of federal money. Notable examples of this influence may be found in the field of river and harbor improvements, the creation of various new bureaus in the Department of Commerce, the enormous extension of the activities of the Agricultural Department and the Bureau of Education. The temptation in this direction is particularly strong among the less prosperous states, for it means the expenditure in those states of federal moneys raised chiefly from the taxpayers in wealthier states.

The most potent influence of all, however, has been the matter of internal economic development, stimulated by free trade among the states. This development has gone on apace with little regard for state lines. The invention of railways drew the different sections of the country together in a common growth, and tended to make the barriers interposed by state lines and state laws seem artificial and cumbersome. In fact, they sometimes came to be regarded as intolerable and destructive of progress. The spectacle of men clamoring for federal control of their industries to escape the burdens of a diversified state interference has been a frequent phenomenon of recent years.[24]

The foregoing enumeration by no means covers all the forces which have been at work. In recent years a strong tendency toward centralization and combination has developed, a tendency pervading all the interests and activities of men. Moreover, new views have arisen concerning the functions and scope of government, views challenging the *"laissez faire"* doctrines of earlier days and demanding a greater measure of governmental interference with the affairs of the individual. These tendencies, however, are not peculiar to America and lie outside the scope of the present discussion.

In considering the methods by which the change of spirit toward the Constitution has been put into effect, one is struck by the comparatively small part played by the only method contemplated by the framers, viz., constitutional amendment. This method is entirely practicable and fairly expeditious provided a sufficient number favor the change proposed. In the one hundred years prior to the recent Income Tax Amendment, however, only three amendments were enacted (Numbers XIII, XIV, and XV), all of them dealing primarily with the abolition of slavery and the civil rights of the Negro. The only one which need be noticed here is Number XIV, which substituted a federal test of citizenship for state tests and provided that no state should "deprive any person of life, liberty, or property, without due process of law; nor deny to any person within its jurisdiction the equal protection of the laws." There was nothing new in these prohibitions. In substance they are as old as Magna Charta and were already embodied in most if not all of the state constitutions. The novelty lay in bringing the question, whether a state had in fact denied due process of law to an

---

[24] See e.g. the efforts of the life insurance interests: N.Y. Life Ins. Co. v. Deer Lodge County, 231 U.S., 495

individual or corporation, within the jurisdiction of the federal courts. From a legal viewpoint this was a change of great importance. To the general student of constitutional government, however, it is less significant than others presently to be mentioned.

Right here it may be proper to notice a new theory of construction of the Constitution, not yet accepted but strenuously urged and containing enormous potentialities. This is the "doctrine of sovereign and inherent power," i.e., the doctrine that powers of national scope for whose exercise no express warrant is found in the Constitution are nevertheless to be implied as inherent in the very fact of sovereignty. This is a very different thing from the famous doctrine of implied powers developed by Chief Justice Marshall--that all powers will be implied which are suitable for carrying into effect any power expressly granted. It is a favorite theory of what may be termed the Roosevelt school. They consider that it is rendered necessary by the discovery of fields suitable for legislative cultivation, lying outside the domain of state power but not within the scope of any express grant of power to the nation. As practical men they abhor the existence of such a constitutional no man's land as nature abhors a vacuum.

During the presidency of Mr. Roosevelt a determined effort was made by the representatives of the Administration[25] to secure the recognition by the Supreme Court of the doctrine of sovereign and inherent power. It was claimed in the brief filed by the Attorney General and Solicitor General that the doctrine had already been applied by the Court in the Legal Tender cases.[26] The effort failed, however, the Court declaring that any such power, if necessary to the nation, must be conferred through constitutional amendment by the people, to whom all powers not granted had been expressly reserved by the Tenth Amendment.

A method by which the federal power and jurisdiction have been much extended has been the occupation by Congress, through legislation of an exclusive character, of fields where the states had exercised a concurrent jurisdiction. A familiar example is found in federal bankruptcy laws. Another and striking example is the so-called "Carmack Amendment" of the federal Interstate Commerce law. The question of liability for loss or damage to

---

[25] In Kansas v. Colorado, 206 U.S., 46.

[26] Bryce makes a statement to the same effect. "The American Commonwealth," Vol. I, p. 383.

goods in the hands of railways and other carriers had been a fruitful field for state legislatures and state courts. The Carmack Amendment brushed away at a single stroke whole systems of state statutes and judicial decisions (in so far as they affected traffic across state lines) and substituted a uniform system under the control of the federal courts.

The federal power has also been extended at the expense of the states through the use of the treaty-making prerogative. The subjects upon which Congress may legislate are limited by specific enumeration. The treaty-making power, however, is not thus limited. Treaties may cover any subject. It follows that while the Federal Government has no power (for example) to regulate the descent of real property in the various states the treaty-making power permits it, by treaties with foreign nations, to destroy the alienage laws of the states.[27]   Another very recent example is afforded by the Migratory Bird Treaty with Great Britain.[28] One will search the Constitution in vain for any grant of power to the Federal Government to enact game laws. Nevertheless, under this treaty, many state game laws have been practically annulled.

But the most far-reaching method by which federal power under the Constitution has been extended has been the adaptation--some will say the perversion--by Congress of old grants of power to new ends. Under the spur of public sentiment Congress has discovered new legislative possibilities in familiar clauses of the Constitution as one discovers new beauties in a familiar landscape. The clause offering the greatest possibilities has been the so-called Commerce Clause, which grants to Congress power "to regulate commerce with foreign nations, and among the several states."[29] Under this grant of power Congress has enacted, and the courts have upheld, a great mass of social and economic legislation having to do only remotely with commerce. For example, the Sherman Act and other anti trust legislation, ostensibly mere regulations of commerce, but actually designed for the control and suppression of trusts and monopolies; the federal Pure Food and Drugs Act, designed to prevent the adulteration or mis-branding of foods and

---

[27] Hauenstein v. Lynham, 100 U.S., 483.

[28] Sustained by the Supreme Court in Missouri v. Holland, 252 U.S., 416.

[29] Art. I, Sec. 8

drugs and check the abuses of the patent-medicine industry;[30] the act for the suppression of lotteries, making it a crime against the United States to carry or send lottery tickets or advertisements across state lines;[31] an act to prevent the importation of prize fight films.[32] These are only a few among many similar statutes which might be mentioned. In all of them the motive is clear. There is no concealment about it. Their primary object is to suppress or regulate the trusts, lotteries, patent-medicine frauds. The regulation of commerce is merely a matter of words and legal form.

Especially noteworthy is the rapidly expanding body of social legislation--federal Employers' Liability Act, Hours of Service acts, Child Labor Law, White Slave Act and the like, all drawn with an eye to the commerce clause but designed to accomplish objects quite distinct from the regulation of commerce.

As already said, the Commerce Clause has been found most available for purposes of such legislation. Other clauses have, however, served their turn. For example, the grant of power to lay taxes was utilized to destroy an extensive industry obnoxious to the dairy interests--the manufacture of oleomargarine artificially colored to look like butter,[33] also to invade the police power of the States in respect of the regulation of the sale and use of narcotic drugs.[34]   Also to check speculation and extortion in the sale of theatre tickets![35] The power to borrow money and create fiscal agencies was utilized to facilitate the making of loans upon farm security at low rates of interest through the incorporation of Federal land banks or Joint Stock land banks.[36]

It would be an insult to intelligence to claim that legislation such as this, wearing the form of revenue measure or regulation of commerce but in reality enacted with a different motive, does not involve an enormous

---

[30] Hipolite Egg Company v. United States, 220 U.S., 45.

[31] Champion v. Ames, 188 U.S., 321.

[32] Weber v. Freed, 239 U.S., 325.

[33] McCray v. United States, 195 U.S., 27.

[34] Narcotic Drug Act. Held constitutional in United States v. Doremus, 249 U.S., 86; Webb v. United States, 249 U.S., 96.

[35] Revenue Act of 1921, Title VIII, subdivisions 2 and 3

[36] Smith v. Kansas City Title Co, 255 U.S., 180

extension of the national power beyond what the makers of the Constitution supposed they were conferring or intended to confer. What, then, of the declaration by the Supreme Court with which we began, that "to determine the extent of the grants of power we must place ourselves in the position of the men who framed and adopted the Constitution, and inquire what they must have understood to be the meaning and scope of these grants." The answer must be that the Court itself has not always adhered strictly to this test. The Court has taken the position that when power exists under the Constitution to legislate upon a given subject--say interstate commerce or taxation--it is not for the judiciary to seek to correct abuses by Congress of that power, or to question Congressional motives. As said in the decision sustaining the constitutionality of the oleomargarine law:[37]

> "The judiciary is without authority to avoid an act of Congress lawfully exerting the taxing power, even in a case where to the judicial mind it seems that Congress had, in putting such power in motion, abused its lawful authority by levying a tax which was unwise or oppressive, or the result of the enforcement of which might be to indirectly affect subjects not within the powers delegated to Congress, nor can the judiciary inquire into the motive or purpose of Congress in adopting a statute levying an excise tax within its constitutional power. "

The Court, however, has had great difficulty with these cases and developed sharp differences of opinion. For example, the case upholding the anti-lottery statute as a valid exercise of the power to regulate commerce[38] was twice ordered for reargument and finally decided by a bare majority of 5 to 4. The Child Labor Law of 1916 was declared unconstitutional[39] and the Narcotic Drug Act was sustained[40] by a similar vote, 5 to 4. In the Narcotic Drug case the four dissenting justices, speaking through Chief Justice White, characterized portions of the statute as "beyond the constitutional power of Congress to enact ... a mere attempt by Congress to exert a power not

---

[37] McCray v. United States, 195 U.S., 27

[38] Champion v. Ames, 188 U.S., 321.

[39] Hammer v. Dagenhart, 247 U.S., 251.

[40] United States v. Doremus, 249 U.S., 86.

delegated, that is, the reserved police power of the states." In the Lottery case the dissenting opinion of the four, written by Chief Justice Fuller, concludes:

> *"I regard this decision as inconsistent with the views of the framers of the Constitution, and of Marshall, its great expounder. Our form of government may remain notwithstanding legislation or decision, but, as long ago observed, it is with governments, as with religions, the form may survive the substance of the faith. "*

Whatever view one may hold to-day as to the question of expediency, no thoughtful mind can escape the conclusion that, in a very real and practical sense, the Constitution has changed. In a way change is inevitable to adapt it to the conditions of the new age. There is danger, however, that in the process of change something may be lost; that present-day impatience to obtain desired results by the shortest and most effective method may lead to the sacrifice of a principle of vital importance.

The men who framed the Constitution were well advised when they sought to preserve the integrity of the states as a barrier against the aggressions and tyranny of the majority acting through a centralized power. The words "state sovereignty" acquired an odious significance in the days of our civil struggle, but the idea for which they stand is nevertheless a precious one and represents what is probably America's most valuable contribution to the science of government.

We shall do well not to forget the words of that staunch upholder of national power and authority, Salmon P. Chase, speaking as Chief Justice of the Supreme Court in a famous case growing out of the Civil War:[41]

> *"The preservation of the states, and the maintenance of their governments, are as much within the design and care of the Constitution as the preservation of the Union and the maintenance of the National Government. The Constitution, in all its provisions, looks to an indestructible Union composed of indestructible states. "*

---

[41] Texas v. White, 7 Wall., 700.

Salmon Portland Chase (January 13, 1808 – May 7, 1873) was an American politician and jurist who served as U.S. Senator from Ohio and the 23rd Governor of Ohio; as U.S. Treasury Secretary under President Abraham Lincoln; and as Chief Justice of the United States. Upon Roger B. Taney's death, Lincoln nominated him as the Chief Justice of the United States, which Chase held from 1864 until his own death in 1873.

Chapter IV
THE EIGHTEENTH AMENDMENT

Could Washington, Madison, and the other framers of the Federal Constitution revisit the earth in this year of grace 1922, it is likely that nothing would bewilder them more than the recent Prohibition Amendment. Railways, steamships, the telegraph, the telephone, automobiles, flying machines, submarines--all these developments of science, unknown in their day, would fill them with amazement and admiration. They would marvel at the story of the rise and downfall of the German Empire; at the growth and present greatness of the Republic they themselves had founded. None of these things, however, would seem to them to involve any essential change in the beliefs and purposes of men as they had known them. The Prohibition Amendment, on the contrary, would evidence to their minds the breaking down of a principle of government which they had deemed axiomatic, the abandonment of a purpose which they had supposed immutable. As students of the science of government they would realize that the most fundamental change which can overtake a free people is a change in their frame of mind, for to that everything else must sooner or later conform. The amendment was proposed by Congress in 1917 and proclaimed as having been ratified in 1919.[42]

The comparative ease and dispatch with which it was put through argue alike the skill and vigor of its sponsors and the strength of the sentiment behind them. Legal warfare over the amendment did not end, however, with its ratification by the legislatures of the requisite number of states. Passions had been aroused. Vast property interests were menaced. Moreover, in the minds of students of government the amendment stirred misgivings which were quite independent of the sentimental and material considerations involved. Eminent counsels were retained and a determined effort was made to defeat or nullify the amendment in the courts. To this end suits were begun in various jurisdictions to test its validity and enjoin the enforcement of the Volstead Act, which sought to carry it into effect. Two sovereign states (Rhode Island and New Jersey) joined in the attack and through their respective Attorneys General brought original suits in the United States Supreme Court to have the amendment declared invalid. Seven

---

[42] 40 Stat. 1050, 1941.

test cases were argued together in the Supreme Court, five days in all being devoted to the argument. It will be of interest to note some of the reasons advanced against the validity of the amendment, as they are summarized in the official report.[43]

The Attorney General of the State of Rhode Island argued[44] that:

> "The amendment is an invasion of the sovereignty of the complaining state and her people, not contemplated by the amending clause of the Constitution. The amending power ... is not a substantive power but a precautionary safeguard inserted incidentally to insure the ends set forth in that instrument against errors and oversights committed in its formation. Amendments, as the term indeed implies, are to be limited to the correction of such errors....
>
> "It is "This Constitution" that may be amended. "This Constitution" is not a code of transient laws but a framework of government and an embodiment of fundamental principles. By an amendment, the identity or purpose of the instrument is not to be changed; its defects may be cured, but "This Constitution" must remain. It would be the greatest absurdity to contend that there was a purpose to create a limited government and at the same time to confer upon that government a power to do away with its own limitations."

The Attorney General of the State of New Jersey:[45]

> "..attacked the amendment as "an invasion of state sovereignty not authorized by the amending clause and as not, properly speaking, an amendment, but legislation, revolutionary in character."

---

[43] National Prohibition cases, 253 U.S., 350

[44] Ibid., pp. 354-356.

[45] 253 U.S., pp. 356-357

The eminent Chicago lawyer, Levy Mayer, and ex-Solicitor General William Marshall Bullitt, contended,[46] among other things, that:

> "The power of "amendment" contained in Art. V does not authorize the invasion of the sovereign powers expressly reserved to the states and the people by the Ninth and Tenth Amendments, except with the consent of **ALL** the states.... If amendment under Art. V were unlimited, three fourths of the legislatures would have it in their power to establish a state religion and prohibit free exercise of other religious beliefs; to quarter a standing army in the houses of citizens; to do away with trial by jury and republican form of government; to repeal the provision for a president; and to abolish this court and with it the whole judicial power vested by the Constitution."

Elihu Root, preeminent as a constitutional lawyer, appeared as counsel in one of the test cases. His main contention was summarized in his brief as follows:[47]

> "(a) That the authority to amend the Constitution is a continuance of the constitution-making power and as such is a power quite different and altogether distinct from the law-making power under the Constitution.
> (b) That a grant of the one power does not include or imply a grant of the other.
> (c) That the natural and ordinary meaning of the words used in Article V of the Constitution [the article providing for amendment] limits the power granted to the function of constitution-making as distinguished from ordinary law-making.
> (d) That the purposes of the grant imply the same limitation.

---

[46] Ibid., pp. 357-361.

[47] For the Reporter's Summary see 253 U.S., pp. 361-367.

(e) That other parts of the Constitution--notably Article I--express the same limitation.

(f) That the existence of authority under Article V to enact ordinary laws regulating the conduct of private citizens under color of amendment would be so in conflict with the fundamental principles and spirit of the Constitution that such a construction is not permissible.

There were other arguments of a more technical character. Article V of the Constitution provides that the Congress shall propose amendments "whenever two-thirds of both Houses shall deem it necessary." It was urged that this required the affirmative vote of two-thirds of the entire membership of both Houses, and that two-thirds of a quorum was not sufficient. It was also urged that the proposal was fatally defective because it did not on its face declare that both Houses deemed the amendment necessary. It was also argued that the amendment had not been effectively ratified in certain of the states where it had been approved by the state legislature (notably Ohio) because under the constitutions of those states it was subject to a referendum to the people before becoming effective. The Supreme Court of Ohio had so decided[48] and a referendum had actually been held in that state, resulting in a rejection of the amendment by popular vote. Various arguments were also advanced based on the puzzling phraseology of Section 2 of the amendment that "the Congress and the several States shall have "concurrent power" to enforce this article by appropriate legislation." The eminent constitutional lawyer, W.D. Guthrie, addressed himself particularly to this phase of the controversy.[49] It was urged with much force that the effect of these words was to save the rights of the states, in respect of intrastate matters, by requiring their concurrence in any legislation of Congress regulating such matters.

All the arguments advanced were alike unavailing. The nine members of the Supreme Court were unanimous in sustaining the validity of the amendment, holding that it "by lawful proposal and ratification, has become a part of the Constitution, and must be respected and given effect the same

---

[48] See Hawke v. Smith, 253 U.S., 221.

[49] 253 U.S., pp. 368-380.

as other provisions of that instrument."[50] The Court, however, adopted the very unusual course of deciding the various cases before it (affirming four, reversing one, and dismissing the original bills filed by the states of Rhode Island and New Jersey) without any written opinion. Speaking through Mr. Justice Van Devanter, the Court merely announced its conclusions. This was an unprecedented procedure in a case involving constitutional questions of such importance. It drew criticism from some of the members of the Court itself. Chief Justice White said:[51]

> "I profoundly regret that in a case of this magnitude, affecting as it does an amendment to the Constitution dealing with the powers and duties of the national and state governments, and intimately concerning the welfare of the whole people, the court has deemed it proper to state only ultimate conclusions without an exposition of the reasoning by which they have been reached...."

and proceeded to announce the reasons which had actuated him personally.

Justice McKenna said:[52]
> "The court declares conclusions only, without giving any reasons for them. The instance may be wise--establishing a precedent now, hereafter wisely to be imitated. It will undoubtedly decrease the literature of the court if it does not increase lucidity."

Perhaps a hint as to the reasons actuating the majority of the Court may be found in the brief concurring memorandum of Mr. Justice McReynolds.
He said:[53]
> "I do not dissent from the disposition of these causes as ordered by the Court, but confine my concurrence to that. It is impossible now to say with fair certainty what construction should be given to the

---

[50] Ibid., p. 386.

[51] Ibid., p. 388.

[52] 253 U.S., p. 393.

[53] Ibid., p. 392.

Eighteenth Amendment. Because of the bewilderment which it creates, a multitude of questions will inevitably arise and demand solution here. In the circumstances, I prefer to remain free to consider these questions when they arrive. "

Justices McKenna and Clarke dissented from portions of the decision dealing with the question of the proper construction of the grant of "concurrent power" to Congress and the States, and wrote opinions setting forth the grounds of their dissent. Both Justices, however, concurred in affirming the validity of the amendment.

Thus the legal battle was fought and lost. The amendment had withstood attack and men's minds settled back to the practical question of its enforcement. Upon that question, however difficult and interesting, we do not here enter. Our present concern is to ascertain as nearly as may be the true place of the amendment in the development of American constitutional law.

That it affords startling evidence of a radical departure from the views of the founders of the Republic is beyond question. Such a blow at the prerogatives of the states, such a step toward centralization, would have been thought impossible by the men of 1787. It would be a mistake, however, to view the departure as having originated with this amendment. Rather is the amendment to be regarded as merely a spectacular manifestation of a change which was already well under way.

In the early days of the Republic the dominating purpose was the protection of state prerogatives, so far as that was compatible with the common safety. The first eleven amendments of the Federal Constitution were all limitations upon federal power. Not until the people of the various states had been drawn together and taught to think in terms of the nation by a great Civil War was there any amendment which enlarged the powers of the National Government. The three post-war amendments (Nos. XIII, XIV, and XV) marked a distinct expansion of federal power but one that seemed to find its justification, as it found its origin, in the necessity for effectuating the purposes of the war and protecting the newly enfranchised Negroes.

A long period of seeming inactivity, more than forty years, elapsed before another constitutional amendment was adopted.[54] The inaction, however, was apparent rather than real. As matter of fact, a change was all the time going on. In a very real sense the Constitution was being altered almost from year to year. That the alterations did not take the shape of formal written amendments was largely due to the tradition of constitutional immobility. The idea had grown up that the machinery of amendment provided by the Fathers was so slow and cumbersome that it was impossible as a practical matter to secure a change by that method except under stress of war or great popular excitement. That idea is now exploded. We of to-day know better, having seen the Income Tax Amendment (No. XVI), the Election of Senators by Popular Vote Amendment (No. XVII), the Prohibition Amendment (No. XVIII), and the Woman Suffrage Amendment (No. XIX) go through within a period of seven years. For generations, however, the tradition of constitutional immobility held sway and the forces of change worked through channels that seemed easier and less obstructed.

The principal channel has been congressional legislation. Congress has found ways of reaching by indirection objects which could not be approached directly. Under the express grants of power contained in the Constitution statutes have been enacted which were really designed to accomplish some ulterior object. A striking example is found in the child labor laws, discussed more at length in a subsequent chapter. Congress at first sought to regulate child labor by a statute enacted ostensibly as a regulation of commerce under the Commerce Clause of the Constitution. The Supreme Court held the Act unconstitutional as exceeding the commerce power of Congress and invading the powers reserved to the states.[55] Thereupon Congress practically reenacted it, coupled with a provision for a prohibitive tax on the profits of concerns employing child labor, as part of a revenue act enacted under the constitutional grant of power to lay taxes.[56]

The assumption by the National Government of jurisdiction over the manufacture and sale of intoxicating liquors is no more of an encroachment on the prerogatives of the states than is its assumption of jurisdiction over child labor and the use of narcotic drugs. We come back, therefore, to the

---

[54] No. XVI, the Income Tax Amendment, ratified in 1913.

[55] Hammer v. Dagenhart, 247 U.S., 251.

[56] Revenue Act of 1918, Title XII.

proposition that the Prohibition Amendment is to be regarded less as a departure in American fundamental law than as a spectacular manifestation of a change already well under way.

The change, however much students of our institutions may deplore it, is not difficult to explain. The earlier solicitude for state rights was in a sense accidental. It was based on sentiment and mutual jealousies among the colonies rather than on any fundamental differences in race, beliefs, or material interests. The traditions behind it, while strong, were of comparatively recent growth. When they entered the Union the colonies were still new and undeveloped. As men died and their sons succeeded them prejudices gradually yielded and sentiment changed. Moreover, various other forces--immigration, free trade among the states, the growth of railways and other nationwide industries, foreign wars--have been at work to obliterate state lines.

Advocates of the old order see in the change a breaking down of the principle of local self government. To their minds the danger of majority tyranny, made possible by a centralization of power in a republic of such vast extent and varied interests, outweighs all the advantages of national uniformity and efficiency. Advocates of the new order think otherwise. They argue, moreover, that the states have become too great and populous to serve as units for purposes of home rule; that their boundaries are for the most part artificial and correspond to no real distinctions in the ordinary life of men. They assert that the instinct for local self-government remains as strong as it ever was, and instance the resentment of New York City over interference from Albany.

The average man gives little thought to the constitutional aspect of the controversy. His interest in the prohibition movement is focused on other features which seem to him of more immediate concern. And yet, did he but realize it, the constitutional aspect transcends all the others in its importance for the future welfare and happiness of himself, his children, and his country.

Chapter V
THE NINETEENTH AMENDMENT

A prudent man touches the question of woman suffrage gingerly. Many fingers have been burnt in that fire and its embers are not yet dead. Some mention of the Nineteenth Amendment seems necessary, however, in any discussion of federal encroachment on state power, and it may be possible to approach the suffrage movement from the standpoint of constitutional law without getting upon controversial ground.

The United States Constitution as originally adopted did not prescribe who should be entitled to vote. That matter was left entirely in the hands of the states. The Constitution provided[57] that, for the election of members of the House of Representatives, "the electors in each state shall have the qualifications requisite for electors of the most numerous branch of the state legislature." It was further provided that Senators should be chosen by the legislatures of the states[58] and that the President and Vice-president should be chosen by presidential electors appointed in such manner as the state legislatures might direct.[59] These were the only elective federal officials.

While the states were thus left in full control, it does not follow that the matter was deemed wholly outside the proper scope of national authority. No argument is necessary to demonstrate that the regulation of the suffrage in national elections is or may be a matter of national concern. The question of prescribing the qualifications of voters in such elections was much debated in the Convention which framed the Constitution.[60] Some members were in favor of prescribing a property qualification and limiting the suffrage to freeholders. It was finally decided, however, to accept the qualifications prescribed by state law. In adopting this plan the Convention followed the line of least resistance. The qualifications of voters in the

---

[57] Article I, Section 2

[58] Article I, Section 3

[59] Article II, Section 1

[60] See e.g., Farrand, "Records of the Federal Convention," Vol. II, p. 201 et seq.

various states differed.[61] Most states required a property qualification, but some did not. It was felt that to attempt to impose a uniform rule on all the states would arouse opposition and create one more obstacle to be overcome in the formidable task of getting the Constitution ratified.

There the matter rested, with suffrage qualifications regulated entirely by state law, until after the Civil War. Meanwhile, the states had been abolishing property tests, and universal male suffrage had been written into state constitutions. The cry for woman suffrage had begun, but as yet it was only a still small voice, inaudible to legislators.

After the Civil War the problem of protecting the emancipated slaves had to be dealt with, and three constitutional amendments (Nos. XIII, XIV, and XV) were adopted with that end primarily in view. Number XIII, ratified in 1865, formally abolished slavery. Number XIV, ratified in 1868, extended citizenship to all persons born in the United States and provided (among other things) that no state should abridge the privileges or immunities of citizens of the United States. Number XV, ratified in 1870, provided that "the right of citizens of the United States to vote shall not be denied or abridged by the United States or by any State on account of race, color, or previous condition of servitude." Here was the entering wedge of federal interference. The amendments did not purport to deal with woman suffrage, but the pioneers of the suffrage movement thought they discovered in them a means of advancing their cause and lost no time in putting the matter to the test. Susan B. Anthony voted at Rochester, N.Y., in an election for a representative in Congress, claiming that the restriction of voting to males by the constitution and laws of New York was void as a violation of the Fourteenth Amendment providing that "no state shall make or enforce any law which shall abridge the privileges or immunities of citizens of the United States." She was indicted for voting unlawfully, and on her trial before Justice Hunt of the United States Supreme Court, sitting at Circuit, the Court directed the jury to find a verdict of guilty and imposed a fine of $100 and costs.[62]

Mrs. Virginia Minor raised a similar question in the courts of Missouri. The Missouri constitution limited the right to vote to male citizens.

---

[61] For a statement of the qualifications in the various states see Minor v. Happersett, 21 Wall., 162

[62] United States v. Anthony, 11 Blatchford, 200

Mrs. Minor applied for registration as a voter, and on being refused brought suit against the Registrar of Voters on the ground that this clause of the Missouri constitution was in violation of the Fourteenth Amendment. The Missouri state courts decided against her, and the case was taken to the Supreme Court of the United States where the decision of the state courts was affirmed.[63] The Supreme Court held in effect that while Mrs. Minor was a citizen that fact alone did not make her a voter; that suffrage was not coextensive with citizenship, either when the Constitution was adopted or at the date of the Fourteenth Amendment, and was not one of the "privileges and immunities" guaranteed by that amendment.

A similar decision was rendered in the matter of Mrs. Myra Bradwell's application for a license to practise law in Illinois.[64] The Supreme Court held that the right to practise law in the state courts was not a privilege or immunity of a citizen of the United States within the meaning of the Fourteenth Amendment, and affirmed the decision of the Illinois Court denying Mrs. Bradwell's application.

The failure of these attempts to turn the Fourteenth Amendment to the advantage of the woman suffrage movement in no wise checked the movement or discouraged its leaders. They redoubled their efforts among the separate states, and worked to such good purpose that the opposition presently began to take on the aspect of a forlorn hope. "Votes for Women" became an accomplished fact in many states, and appeared on the verge of accomplishment in most of the others. Some states, however, were still holding out when the leaders of the movement, impatient of further delay and determined to coerce the recalcitrants, took the matter into the national arena and procured the proposal and ratification of an amendment to the Federal Constitution. The amendment provides:

> *"The right of citizens of the United States to vote shall not be denied or abridged by the United States or by any state on account of sex."*

---

[63] Minor v. Happersett, 21 Wall., 162.

[64] Bradwell v. Illinois, 16 Wall., 130.

In other words, it adopts verbatim the phraseology of the Fifteenth Amendment, merely substituting the word "sex" for the words "race, color, or previous condition of servitude."

So much for the historical background of the so-called Susan B. Anthony Amendment. It remains to consider just how far the amendment constitutes an encroachment by the Federal Government on the powers of the states.

In so far as it affects the qualifications of voters at national elections (i.e., for president, senators, representatives) the encroachment is more apparent than real. As has already been pointed out, this is essentially a national question, and the Constitution adopted the suffrage qualifications prescribed by state law, not as a matter of principle, but for reasons of expediency and convenience.

In so far, however, as the amendment imposes woman suffrage on the states in elections of state and local officials the situation is entirely different. That staunch advocate of national power, Alexander Hamilton, said in the "*Federalist*":[65]

> "*Suppose an article had been introduced into the Constitution,*
> *empowering the United States to regulate the elections for*
> *theparticular states, would any man have hesitated to condemn it,*
> *both as an unwarrantable transposition of power, and as a*
> *premeditated engine for the destruction of the state governments?* "

What Hamilton scouted as impossible has been accomplished in the Nineteenth Amendment. It in effect strikes out the word "male" from the suffrage provisions of state constitutions. It overrides state policy and interferes with the right of states to manage their own affairs. From the theoretical standpoint a more serious inroad on state prerogatives would be hard to find. Control of the suffrage is one of the fundamental rights of a free state. It belonged to the North American states before their union, and was not surrendered to the National Government when the union was effected.

---

[65] Federalist LIX

Moreover, the encroachment has a very practical side. To confer the suffrage on the educated women of Connecticut was one thing; to confer it on the Negro women of Alabama was quite a different matter, involving different considerations. The amendment took no heed of such differences but imposed a uniform rule on all the states, regardless of local prejudices or conditions.

It is true that a somewhat similar encroachment on state power had been made by the Fifteenth Amendment, designed to enfranchise the Negroes. That amendment, however, had its origin in conditions growing out of the Civil War, and claimed its justification in the necessity for protecting the freed slaves against hostile state action. It was avowedly an emergency measure, and the success with which it has been nullified in some quarters testifies to the unwisdom of forcing such measures upon reluctant states.

The conditions surrounding the adoption of the Nineteenth Amendment were altogether different. Few people take seriously the alleged analogy between the women and the slaves. The constitutional method-- action through the separate states--was being pursued with signal success. The states were rapidly falling in line. Most of them had already granted woman suffrage or were ready to grant it. There was no overmastering need for coercing the states that were not yet ready. An impartial student of the period will be apt to conclude that the Nineteenth Amendment was the product of impatience rather than necessity.

Someone may ask, "What effect will the granting of votes to women have on the problem of preserving the constitutional equilibrium?" The ultimate power lies with the voters, and the women with votes now equal or outnumber the men. What is the reaction of women voters likely to be toward questions of political theory?

Ours is a governmental scheme of extreme complexity. As with animal organisms so with political systems, the higher they rise in the scale of development the more complicated they tend to become. An absolute monarchy is simplicity itself compared with our dual system. To maintain the proper adjustment of such a machine requires intelligence of a high order. The machine will not run itself and male tinkers have abundantly demonstrated that it is not fool-proof. But something more is required than mere intelligence. There must be, at least among the leaders, an instinct for governmental problems as distinguished from those of a merely social or personal character; an ability to recognize and a willingness to conform to underlying principles.

How will the women voters meet this test? Granting (what few will dispute) that their intelligence at least equals that of the men, will they be as likely as men to look beyond the immediate social welfare problem to the governmental principle at stake? Will an abstract proposition hold its own in their minds against a concrete appeal?

We do not attempt to answer these questions, but they contain food for thought.

Susan B. Anthony

Susan Brownell Anthony (February 15, 1820 – March 13, 1906) was a prominent American civil rights leader who played a pivotal role in the 19th century women's rights movement to introduce women's suffrage into the United States. She traveled the United States, and Europe, and gave 75 to 100 speeches every year on women's rights for 45 years.

After retiring in 1900, Anthony remained in Rochester, where she died of heart disease and pneumonia in her house at 17 Madison Street on March 13, 1906. She was buried at Mount Hope Cemetery. Following her death, the New York State Senate passed a resolution remembering her "unceasing labor, undaunted courage and unselfish devotion to many philanthropic purposes and to the cause of equal political rights for women."

Chapter VI
CONGRESS VERSUS THE SUPREME COURT--THE CHILD LABOR LAWS

The present Federal Revenue Act is noteworthy in more aspects than its complexity and the disproportionate burden cast on possessors of great wealth. To students of our form of government it is particularly interesting because of provisions[66] purporting to impose a tax on employers of child labor, for these represent an attempt by Congress to nullify a decision of the Supreme Court and grasp a power belonging to the states. The story of these provisions throws a flood of light on a method by which our Constitution is being changed.

The evils of child labor have long engaged the attention of philanthropists and lawmakers. In comparatively recent years child labor laws are said to have been enacted in every state of the Union. These statutes, however, lacked uniformity. Some of them were not stringent enough to satisfy modern sentiment. Moreover, commercial considerations entered into the reckoning. Industries in states where the laws were stringent were found to be at a disadvantage in comparison with like industries in states where the laws were lax, and this came to be regarded as a species of unfair competition. The advantages of uniformity and standardization seemed obvious from both the philanthropic and the commercial viewpoints, and Congress determined to take a hand in the matter.

No well-informed person supposed for a moment that the regulation of child labor was one of the functions of the General Government as those functions were planned by the makers of the Constitution. The United States Supreme Court had declared over and over again that such matters were the province of the states; that "speaking generally, the police power is reserved to the states and there is no grant thereof to Congress in the Constitution."[67] For some years, however, Congress had been finding ways to legislate indirectly upon matters which it had no power to approach directly. Under

---

[66] Revenue Act of 1921, Title XII.

[67] Keller v. United States, 213 U.S., 138.

the grant of power in the Constitution "to regulate commerce with foreign nations and among the several States,"[68]   Congress had enacted laws purporting to regulate commerce but in reality designed for the suppression or regulation of some other form of activity. These enactments had for the most part been sustained as constitutional by the Supreme Court (though with misgivings and sharp differences of opinion), the Court holding that it could not pass on the motives for congressional action. The enactment of a law regulating child labor seemed therefore but another step along a trail already blazed, and Congress determined to take that step.

The statute enacted by Congress[69] prohibited transportation in interstate commerce of goods made at a factory in which, within thirty days prior to their removal therefrom, children under the age of fourteen years had been employed or permitted to work, or children between the ages of fourteen and sixteen had been employed or permitted to work more than eight hours in any day, or more than six days in any week, or after the hour of 7 P.M. or before the hour of 6 A.M. The constitutionality of the act was at once challenged and suit brought to test the question. The Supreme Court held, by a vote of five to four,[70] that Congress had overstepped its power. The previous decisions which had upheld somewhat similar inroads on the police power of the states were distinguished and the act was declared unconstitutional.

The distinction drawn by the majority of the Court between this and previous decisions was a narrow one and its validity has been questioned by some writers. It has nowhere been more clearly explained than in an address delivered before a body of lawyers by a former member of the Court.[71] Mr. Hughes said:

> "There has been in late years a series of cases sustaining the
> regulation of interstate commerce, although the rules established by
> Congress had the quality of police regulation. This has been decided
> with respect to the interstate transportation of lottery tickets, of

---

[68] Art. I, Sec. 8.

[69] Act of September 1, 1916, 39 Stat., 675.

[70] Hammer v. Dagenhart, 247 U.S., 251.

[71] Charles E. Hughes, President's Address, Printed in Year Book of New York State Bar Association, Vol. XLII, p. 227 et seq.

impure food and drugs, of misbranded articles, of intoxicating liquors, and of women for the purpose of debauchery. It was held to be within the power of Congress to keep "the channels of interstate commerce free from immoral and injurious uses." But the Court in this most recent decision has pointed out that in each of these cases "the use of interstate commerce was necessary to the accomplishment of harmful results." The Court, finding this element to be wanting in the Child Labor Case, denied the validity of the act of Congress. The Court found that the goods shipped were of themselves harmless. They were permitted to be freely shipped after thirty days from the time of removal from the factory. The labor of production, it was said, had been performed before transportation began and thus before the goods became the subject of interstate commerce.

"The fundamental proposition thus established is that the power over interstate commerce is not an absolute power of prohibition, but only one of regulation, and that the prior decisions in which prohibitory rules had been sustained rested upon the character of the particular subjects there involved. It was held that the authority over interstate commerce was to regulate such commerce and not to give Congress the power to control the states in the exercise of their police power over local trade and manufacture."

Congress did not receive this decision of the Supreme Court submissively. On the contrary, plans were laid to nullify it. The effort to legislate on child labor under cover of the power to regulate commerce having failed, recourse was had to the constitutional grant of power to lay taxes. Within six months after the decision of the Supreme Court declaring the act unconstitutional was announced, another statute similar in purpose and effect was enacted as part of a Federal Revenue Act.[72] This act provided for an additional tax of ten per cent. of the net profits received from the sale or distribution of the product of any establishment in which children under the age of fourteen years had been employed or permitted to work or children between the ages of fourteen and sixteen had been employed or

---

[72] Revenue Act of 1918, Title XII.

permitted to work more than eight hours in any day or more than six days in any week or after the hour of 7 P.M. or before the hour of 6 A.M. during any portion of the taxable year. In other words, the law which had been declared void was substantially reenacted, with the substitution of a prohibitive tax for the clause prohibiting transportation in interstate commerce.

There was no pretense that this act was enacted for the purpose of raising revenue. The revenue feature was merely legislative camouflage. To quote the words of Justice Holmes in a recent case,[73] "Congress gave it the appearance of a taxing measure in order to give it a coating of constitutionality."

The debate in the Senate was highly illuminating.[74] Its sponsors admitted that the measure was not expected or intended to produce revenue but was designed to regulate child labor and nullify the decision of the Supreme Court. Senators learned in the law conceded that if this purpose and effect were declared on the face of the act, or were necessarily inferable from its provisions, it must inevitably be declared unconstitutional. Reliance was placed, however, on the facts that the act was entitled "A bill to raise revenue," and that its provisions did not necessarily, on their face, belie this label. It was argued that the Supreme Court would be bound, under its own previous rulings, to treat the act as if it were what it purported on its face to be--a revenue measure--and to ignore common knowledge and senatorial admissions to the contrary. The measure passed the Senate by a substantial majority and was enacted as part of the revenue bill then under consideration, from which it has been carried forward into the present revenue law.

There the matter stands at this writing. A District Court judge has declared the new act unconstitutional but the question has not yet been passed upon by the Supreme Court.

It would be venturesome to attempt to predict what the Supreme Court will do about it. Many constitutional lawyers seem to think that Congress has succeeded in its attempt and that the act will be sustained. Certainly there are strong precedents pointing that way. Three in particular

---

[73] United States v. Jin Fuey Moy, 241 U.S., 394.

[74] See "Congressional Record" of December 18, 1918.

will be relied upon--the Veazie Bank case, the "Oleomargarine case and the Narcotic Drug Act" case.

In the Veazie Bank case[75] the Supreme Court upheld the validity of a so-called tax law whose purpose and effect were to suppress the circulation of notes of the state banks. In the Oleomargarine case[76] the Court upheld a tax whose purpose and effect were to suppress the manufacture and sale of oleomargarine artificially colored to look like butter. In the Narcotic Drug case[77] the Court upheld a tax imposed by the so-called Harrison Act[78] whose purpose was to regulate the sale and use of narcotic drugs. In each of these cases there could be no doubt in the mind of any intelligent man as to the motive for the enactment. The Court has uniformly maintained, however, that

> "When Congress acts within the limits of its constitutional authority, it is not the province of the judicial branch of the Government to question its motives.[79]"

In the Narcotic Drug Act case[80] the Court held:

> "While Congress may not exert authority which is wholly reserved to the states, the power conferred by the Constitution to levy excise taxes, uniform throughout the United States, is to be exercised at the discretion of Congress; and, where the provisions of the law enacted have some reasonable relation to this power, the fact that they may have been impelled by a motive, or may accomplish a purpose, other than the raising of revenue, cannot invalidate them; nor can the fact that they affect the conduct of a business which is subject to regulation by the state police power."

---

[75] Veazie Bank v. Fenno, 8 Wall., 533, decided in 1870.

[76] McCray v. United States, 195 U.S., 27, decided in 1904.

[77] United States v. Doremus, 249 U.S., 86, decided in 1919.

[78] 38 Stat., 785

[79] Smith v. Kansas City Title Company, 255 U.S., 180, 210.

[80] United States v. Doremus, 249 U.S., 86.

It is true that, while the Supreme Court may not question congressional motives, it cannot escape the obligation to construe a statute in the light of its true nature and effect. The Court has said:[81]

> *"The direct and necessary result of a statute must be taken into consideration when deciding as to its validity, even if that result is not in so many words either enacted or distinctly provided for. In whatever language a statute may be framed, its purpose must be determined by its natural and reasonable effect."*

As already indicated, however, the nature and effect of a statute must ordinarily be determined from the form and contents of the act itself, rather than from outside sources, and the measure under consideration purports to be a revenue act.

In the light of the decisions and principles of interpretation to which reference has been made, the case against the constitutionality of the act may seem well-nigh hopeless. The fact remains, however, that Congress has not met the fundamental objection raised by the Supreme Court. The Court declared the former act unconstitutional, not only because it transcended the power of Congress under the particular provision of the Constitution then invoked, viz., the Commerce Clause, but also on the broad ground of state rights, because it "exerts a power as to a purely local matter to which the federal authority does not extend." It is difficult to see how this objection is obviated by reenacting the act as a revenue measure. Under the circumstances perhaps the apprehensive foes of federal encroachment should withhold their lamentations until the Supreme Court has spoken again.[82]

---

[81] Collins v. New Hampshire, 171 U.S., 30.

[82] Since this chapter was put into print the Court has spoken.
In Bailey v. The Drexel Furniture Co (decided May 15, 1922) the Child Labor Tax Law was pronounced unconstitutional. The Court, while conceding that it must interpret the intent and meaning of Congress from the language of the act, held that the act on its face is an attempt to regulate matters of state concern by the use of a so-called tax as a penalty. The opinion of the Court, written by Chief Justice Taft, is an emphatic assertion of the duty and function of the Court to preserve the constitutional equilibrium between nation and states.]

Chapter VII
STATE RIGHTS AND THE SUPREME COURT

A century ago the United States Supreme Court was the bulwark of national power against the assaults and pretensions of the states. To-day it is the defender of the states against the encroachments of national power. Let no one suppose, however, that this is because the Court itself has faced about. On our revolving planet a ship may be sailing toward the sun at sunrise and away from the sun in the afternoon without having changed its course. The Supreme Court has been the most consistent factor in our governmental scheme. While there have been differences of viewpoint between liberal constructionists and strict constructionists among its members, the Court on the whole has steered a fairly straight course. What has really altered is the environment in which the Court moves. The earth has been turning on its axis. The frame of mind of the people who compose states and nation has changed.

At the outset (to cling for a moment to our nautical metaphor) the Court was obliged to put forth on an unknown sea. Its sailing orders under the new Constitution were unique. Precedents, those charts and lighthouses of the judicial mariner, were lacking. Progress was tentative and groping. Little wonder therefore that at first the business of the Court was meager and membership in its body seemed less attractive than membership in the judiciary of a state. Robert Hanson Harrison, one of President Washington's original appointees to the Supreme bench, declined to serve, preferring to accept a state judicial office. John Rutledge, another of the original appointees, resigned after a few months, preferring the position of Chancellor of his native state to which he had been chosen. John Jay, the first Chief Justice, resigned to become Governor of New York, and later declined a reappointment as Chief Justice in words indicating entire lack of faith in the powers and future of the Court.

Nevertheless, the first period of the Court was by no means barren of achievement. A beginning was made. The supremacy of the national authority under the new Constitution was asserted. So stoutly indeed was it maintained in the memorable case of Chisholm v. Georgia[83], that the country was thrown into ferment. The Court had entertained a suit against a sovereign state by a private citizen of another state and rendered a decision in favor of the private citizen. The legislature of the sovereign state concerned (Georgia) responded by a statute denouncing the penalty of death against anyone who should presume to enforce any process upon the judgment within its jurisdiction. The matter was taken up in Congress and resulted in the proposal, and subsequent ratification by the states, of a constitutional amendment designed to prevent such actions in future.[84] It has been the fashion to speak of this incident as a striking example of the recall of judicial decisions. Such indeed it was. The decision did not suit the popular frame of mind and was promptly overruled in the method prescribed by the Constitution. It went a long way, however, toward establishing the Supreme Court as a power to be reckoned with on the side of national supremacy and authority.

Three years later the Court again took occasion to assert the national supremacy in no uncertain fashion. The case was Ware v. Hylton[85] and the Court laid down the proposition that a treaty of the Federal Government (in this case the treaty of peace with Great Britain) nullified previous state laws dealing with the subject matter. It is an interesting circumstance that one of the counsels on the losing side in this case was John Marshall of Virginia, and that this was the only case he ever argued before the tribunal through which he was destined to play so momentous a part in history.

In the annals of the Supreme Court and the development of American constitutional law the name of John Marshall stands preeminent. He was appointed Chief Justice by President John Adams, and took his seat on the Bench at the beginning of the new century (February 4, 1801). He was without judicial experience, but his record in other fields of activity and his well-known Federalist principles pointed him out as a man to be reckoned with and explain the aversion with which he was viewed by Thomas Jefferson, the incoming President. The breach between the President and the Chief Justice was widened by some of the early decisions of the latter

---

[83] 2 Dallas, 419, decided in 1793.

[84] Amendment XI.

[85] 3 Dallas, 199, decided in 1796.

upholding the supremacy of the National Government and the powers of the Supreme Court, notably the famous case of Marbury v. Madison[86], in which was asserted the power of the Court to declare an act of Congress void as in conflict with the Constitution. Some years elapsed, however, before a case was decided which squarely involved a conflict between the powers of the Federal Government and the powers of a state. The issue came up in the case of United States v. Judge Peters[87]. This case involved a conflict of jurisdiction between the federal courts and the authorities of the State of Pennsylvania over the distribution of some prize money. Marshall's decision was a strong assertion of the federal jurisdiction and power. The Governor of Pennsylvania, under sanction of the state legislature, called out the state militia to resist enforcement of the judgment of the Court. Matters were tense for a time and bloodshed seemed imminent but the state finally backed down.

In the following year (1810) came the case of Fletcher v. Peck[88], in which for the first time a statute of a state was held by the Supreme Court to be void as repugnant to the Federal Constitution. The State of Georgia had sought by statute to destroy rights in lands acquired under a previous act. It was held that the statute was unconstitutional as impairing the obligation of contracts within the meaning of the Constitution.

In Martin v. Hunter's Lessee[89] was asserted the right of the Federal Supreme Court to overrule the judgment of a state court on questions arising under the Federal Constitution. The State of Virginia had denied that right and the Supreme Court reversed the judgment of the Virginia Court of Appeals.

In McCulloch v. State of Maryland[90], a case involving an attempt by the State of Maryland to tax the Bank of the United States, Marshall's doctrine of implied powers was elaborated, and the judgment of the state court upholding the tax was reversed.

---

[86] 1 Cranch, 137.

[87] 5 Cranch, 115, decided in 1809.

[88] 6 Cranch, 87.

[89] 1 Wheat., 304 (1816.)

[90] 4 Wheat., 316 (1819).

In the Dartmouth College case[91] the doctrine of the inviolability of contracts against attack by state legislation was further developed. An act of the state legislature of New Hampshire had sought to alter the charter of Dartmouth College, and the New Hampshire courts had upheld the legislature. The Supreme Court reversed the state court and declared the statute unconstitutional under the clause of the Constitution which declares that no state shall make any law impairing the obligation of contracts.

In the great case of Gibbons v. Ogden[92] the Court asserted the paramount jurisdiction of the National Government over interstate commerce. This was one of the most important and far-reaching of all Marshall's decisions. An injunction had been granted by Chancellor Kent and unanimously sustained by the Court of Errors of New York, restraining Gibbons from navigating the Hudson River by steamboats licensed by Congress for the coasting trade on the ground that he was thereby infringing the exclusive right, granted by the legislature of New York, to Robert R. Livingston and Robert Fulton to navigate the waters of the state with vessels moved by steam. The Supreme Court reversed the state courts and held the New York legislation void as an interference with the right of Congress, under the Constitution, to regulate interstate commerce.

These were only a few of that series of great decisions which stand out like mountain peaks on the horizon of our national life. Marshall's judgments transformed a governmental experiment into something assured and permanent. They confirmed the national supremacy and made the Constitution workable.

Marshall is known to history for his work in vindicating the national power under the Constitution. That was the need in his day and he met it with superlative wisdom and skill. It would be a mistake, however, to suppose that he favored federal encroachment upon the powers reserved to the states. On the contrary, he rendered decisions in favor of state rights which would be notable were they not overshadowed by the greater fame of the decisions which went to the building of the nation.

---

[91] Dartmouth College v. Woodward, 4 Wheat., 518 (1819).

[92] 9 Wheat., 1 (1824).

With the passing of Marshall and the accession of Taney as Chief Justice a new chapter opened in the history of the Court. The Federalists had become extinct. Andrew Jackson had come into power and it had fallen to his lot to fill a majority of the seats upon the bench by appointments to vacancies. The result was at once apparent. Two case[93] involving important constitutional questions, which had been argued during Marshall's lifetime but assigned for reargument on account of a division in the Court, were now decided contrary to Marshall's known views and in favor of a strict construction of national powers. Justice Story, Marshall's longtime associate on the bench, dissented strongly in both cases, lamenting the loss of Marshall's leadership and the change in the viewpoint of the Court.

It would serve no useful purpose to enter upon a detailed consideration of the various decisions upon constitutional questions made during the twenty-eight years of Taney's Chief Justiceship. They were marked by great diversity of views among the members of the Court. In some of them, notably the famous Passenger cases,[94] the Court fell into a state reminiscent of the confusion of tongues that arose at the building of the Tower of Babel. The scope of certain of Marshall's decisions was limited.[95] Upon the whole, however, the structure of constitutional law which Marshall had reared was not torn down or greatly impaired. The national supremacy was upheld. Taney and his associates were for the most part patriotic men and eminent lawyers, proud of the Court and its history and anxious to add to its prestige. It is regrettable that the merits of some of them have been so obscured and their memory so clouded by a well-meaning but unfortunate excursion into the field of political passions. In the Dred Scott case[96] they thought to quiet agitation and contribute to the peace of their country by passing judgment upon certain angrily mooted questions of a political character. The effort was a failure and brought upon their heads, and upon Chief Justice Taney in particular, an avalanche of misrepresentation and obloquy.

---

[93] Mayor of New York v. Miln, 11 Peters, 102; Briscoe v. Bank of Kentucky, 11 Peters, 257, decided in 1837.

[94] 7 Howard, 283 (1849).

[95] Not always for the worse: vide the Charles River Bridge case, 11 Peters, 420, imposing salutary restrictions on the doctrine of the Dartmouth College case.

[96] Dred Scott v. Sandford, 19 Howard, 393 (1857).

The suppression of the Great Rebellion brought an enormous increase in the national power and in the popular will to national power. State rights did not loom large in the popular or the legislative mind in reconstruction days. Taney was dead. The Supreme Court had been practically reconstituted by appointments made by President Lincoln and his immediate successors and it seems to have been anticipated that the new Court would take the view of national powers prevailing in Congress and the country at large. In this the popular expectation was doomed to disappointment. The Court displayed an unexpected solicitude for the rights of the states and firmness against federal encroachment. Chief Justice Salmon P. Chase, who had been President Lincoln's war Secretary of the Treasury, went so far as to pronounce unconstitutional some of his own official acts performed under the stress of war.

In the great case of State of Texas v. White[97] the rights of Texas as a sovereign state were asserted, though Texas had joined in the Rebellion and was not represented in the national legislature.

In The Collector v. Day[98] it was held that Congress had no power to tax the salary of a state official.

In the Slaughter House cases[99] an act of the Legislature of Louisiana, granting to a corporation created by it exclusive rights to maintain slaughter houses for the City of New Orleans and other territory, was upheld, as a valid exercise of state police power, against claims that the legislation violated rights secured under the newly adopted amendments to the Federal Constitution (Amendments XIII, XIV, XV). The opinion of the Court delivered by a Northern judge (Miller of Iowa) stands as one of the bulwarks of state authority.

In a series of later cases various reconstruction acts of Congress involving encroachments upon state rights were either held unconstitutional or radically limited in their effect. For example, the decision in United States

---

[97] 7 Wall., 700 (1869).

[98] 11 Wall., 113 (1871).

[99] 16 Wall., 36 (1873).

v. Cruikshank[100] greatly limited the effect of the so-called Federal Enforcement Act. The decision in United States v. Harris[101] declared unconstitutional portions of an act of Congress designed for the suppression of activities of the Ku-Klux variety. In the so-called Civil Rights cases[102] certain provisions of the federal Civil Rights Act, passed in furtherance of the purposes of the new constitutional amendments and designed to secure to persons of color equal enjoyment of the privileges of inns, public conveyances, theatres, etc., were held unconstitutional as an encroachment on the rights of the states.

These are but a few of the many decisions of the Supreme Court in the reconstruction period upholding the rights of the states against attempted federal encroachment arising from the conditions of the Civil War. The nation owes a debt of gratitude to the men who composed the Court at this time for their courage and firmness in the face of popular clamor and passion.

The solicitude of the Court for the rights of the states did not end with the reconstruction period. It has continued down to the present day. In the Income Tax cases[103] the Court held that a tax upon income from bonds of a state municipal corporation was repugnant to the Constitution as a tax upon the borrowing power of the state.

In Keller v. United States[104] the Court declared unconstitutional, as an encroachment on the police power of the states, an act of Congress making it a felony to harbor alien prostitutes, the Court declaring that "speaking generally, the police power is reserved to the states and there is no grant thereof to Congress in the Constitution."

In the Child Labor case[105] the Court held the federal Child Labor Law of 1916 unconstitutional as invading the police power reserved to the states. The Court said:

---

[100] 92 U.S., 542 (1875).

[101] 106 U.S., 629.

[102] 109 U.S., 3.

[103] Pollock v. Farmers Loan & Trust Co, 157 U.S., 429 (1895).]

[104] 213 U.S., 138 (1909).

[105] Hammer v. Dagenhart, 247 U.S., 251 (1918).

"This Court has no more important function than that which devolves upon it the obligation to preserve inviolate the constitutional limitations upon the exercise of authority, federal and state, to the end that each may continue to discharge, harmoniously with the other, the duties entrusted to it by the Constitution.[106] "

How is it then, someone may ask, if the Supreme Court is so zealous in defense of the rights of the states, that those rights are being encroached upon more and more by the National Government? The answer must be that there has been a change in the popular frame of mind. The desire for uniformity, standardization, efficiency, has outgrown the earlier fears of a centralization of power. Congress has found ways, under the constitutional grants of power to lay taxes and regulate interstate commerce, to legislate in furtherance of the popular demands. The Court is not strong enough (no governmental agency which could be devised would be strong enough) to hold back the flood or permanently thwart the popular will. In a government of the people everything has to yield sooner or later to the deliberate wish of the majority.

Some profess to view the recent encroachments of federal power as a triumph of the principles advocated by Alexander Hamilton and John Marshall over the principles of Thomas Jefferson. Such a claim does Hamilton and Marshall an injustice. While they both stood for a strong National Government, neither of them contemplated any encroachment by that government on the principle of local self government in local matters or the police power of the states.

Marshall in one of his most powerful and far-reaching pronouncements in support of the national supremacy[107] speaks of:

"that immense mass of legislation, which embraces everything within the territory of a state not surrendered to the General Government;...

---

[106] An even stronger assertion of state rights is found in the Child Labor Tax Case (Bailey v. The Drexel Furniture Co.) decided May 15, 1922, after this chapter had been put into print.

[107] Gibbons v. Ogden, 9 Wheat., 1, 203, 208.

inspection laws, quarantine laws, health laws of every description ... are component parts of this mass."

Later in the same opinion he refers to:

" the acknowledged power of a state to regulate its police, its domestic trade, and to govern its own citizens.... The power of regulating their own purely internal affairs whether of trading or police."

Hamilton devotes an entire number of the Federalist[108] to combatting the idea that the rights of the states are in danger of being invaded by the General Government. In another place[109] he returns to the idea:

" that there is greater probability of encroachments by the members upon the federal head, than by the federal head upon the members and concludes that it is to be hoped that the people will always take care to preserve the constitutional equilibrium between the general and the state governments."

That hope has failed of realization. The "constitutional equilibrium" of which Hamilton wrote is not being preserved. Some will say that this is an age of progress and we are improving upon Hamilton. Others, however, think we are forgetting the wisdom of the Fathers.

---

[108] Federalist, Number XVII.

[109] Ibid., Number XXXI.

John Marshall

John Marshall (September 24, 1755 – July 6, 1835) was an American jurist and statesman who shaped American constitutional law and made the Supreme Court a center of power. Marshall was Chief Justice of the United States, serving from January 31, 1801, until his death in 1835. He served in the United States House of Representatives from March 4, 1799, to June 7, 1800, and was Secretary of State under President John Adams from June 6, 1800, to March 4, The longest serving Chief Justice in Supreme Court history, Marshall dominated the Court for over three decades (a term outliving his own Federalist Party) and played a significant role in the development of the American legal system. Most notably, he established that the courts are entitled to exercise judicial review, the power to strike down laws that violate the

Chapter VIII
THE FEDERAL TAXING POWER AND THE INCOME TAX AMENDMENT

Had the World War come five years earlier the United States would have been much handicapped and embarrassed in financing its share of the struggle. One of the chief sources of national revenue during and since the war, the income tax, would not have been available. The federal income tax had been declared unconstitutional by the Supreme Court in 1895, and it was not until eighteen years later that the obstacle pointed out by that decision was removed through the adoption of an amendment to the Constitution. The Sixteenth or Income Tax Amendment was proposed by Congress to the legislatures of the several states in 1909 and took effect, having been ratified by three-fourths of the states, in 1913. Declared by its sponsors at the outset to be intended merely as a recourse in case of emergency, the tax authorized by the amendment was at once put into operation and there seems to be little likelihood that it will ever be abandoned.

Without the constitutional amendment no general income tax would be practicable. And yet the amendment conferred no new power of taxation on the National Government. To explain this seeming paradox it will be necessary to consider briefly the scope and limitations of the federal taxing power.

One of the chief defects, perhaps the most vital defect of all, in the Confederation which carried through the Revolutionary War and preceded the Union, was its inability to raise revenue directly by taxation. The Confederation was obliged to call upon the several states to furnish their respective contributions or quotas, and requisitions upon the states encountered delays and sometimes were ignored altogether. There were no effective means of compulsion.

With these facts before them the founders of the Union determined that the new government should not be wrecked upon this rock at any rate, and therefore insisted, against great opposition, in conferring upon it powers of taxation which were practically unlimited in their reach. The Constitution was made to provide that:[110]

> *"the Congress shall have power to lay and collect taxes, duties, imposts and excises, to pay the debts and providethe common defense and general welfare of the United States."*

The only tax which Congress was expressly forbidden to lay was a tax on exports.[111] It was, however, provided that indirect taxes (duties, imposts, and excises) should be uniform throughout the United States,[112] and that direct taxes should be apportioned among the states according to population.[113] The last mentioned provision was a concession to the fears of the wealthier states lest their citizens be taxed unduly for the benefit of the poorer states, and represented one of the great compromises by which the ratification of the Constitution as a whole was secured.

The Constitution nowhere specified just what taxes were to be deemed "direct" (Madison in his notes of the Constitutional Convention records: "Mr. King asked what was the precise meaning of direct taxation? No one answd.")[114] or what kind of uniformity was intended by the provision that indirect taxes should be uniform, and more than a century was to elapse before either of these fundamental questions was finally settled. The answer to the latter question (that the term "uniform" refers purely to a geographical uniformity and is synonymous with the expression "to operate generally throughout the United States") was given by the Supreme Court in the year 1900 in the celebrated case of Knowlton v. Moore, [115] and met with general approval. The answer to the question of what constitutes a direct tax within the meaning of the Constitution, given by the Supreme Court in 1895 in the Income Tax cases,[116] met with a different reception. The decision upset long-settled ideas, disarranged the federal taxing system, aroused popular

---

[110] Const., Art. I, Sec. 8, Clause 1.

[111] Const., Art. I, Sec. 9, Clause 5.

[112] Ibid., Art. I, Sec. 8, Clause 1.

[113] Ibid., Art. I, Sec. 2, Clause 3. Sec. 9, Clause 4.

[114] Farrand, "Records of the Federal Convention," Vol. II, p. 350.

[115] 178 U.S., 41.

[116] Pollock v. Farmers Loan & Trust Co, 157 U.S., 429.

resentment, and ultimately led to the enactment of the Sixteenth Amendment.

The question had arisen early in the life of the Republic in the case of _Hylton v. United States_, decided in 1796.[117] This litigation involved the validity of a tax on carriages which had been imposed by Congress without apportionment among the states. Alexander Hamilton argued the case before the Supreme Court in support of the tax. The Court adopted his view and sustained the tax, holding that it was a tax on consumption and therefore a species of excise or duty. The Justices who wrote opinions expressed doubt whether anything but poll taxes and taxes on land were "direct" within the meaning of the Constitution. That point, however, was not necessarily involved and was not decided, though later generations came to assume that it had been decided.

The tax on carriages was soon repealed and many years elapsed before the question came up again. After the Civil War broke out, however, the need of revenue became acute and various statutes taxing income without apportionment among the states were enacted by Congress. These met with general acquiescence. It was felt that they were emergency measures necessitated by the war, and they were in fact abandoned as soon as practicable after the war. A well-known lawyer, however (William M. Springer of Illinois), did not acquiesce and refused to pay his income tax, on the ground that it was a direct tax not levied in accordance with the Constitution. In the action brought to test the question[118] it appeared that the income on which Mr. Springer had been taxed was derived in part from the practice of his profession as an attorney. To this extent it was clearly an excise or duty, i.e., an indirect tax. As it was incumbent upon Mr. Springer, by reason of the form of the action, to demonstrate that the tax was void _in toto_ the Court could not do otherwise than decide against him. In rendering its decision, however, the Court took occasion to discuss the question as to what were direct taxes within the meaning of the Constitution, and expressed the view that the term included only capitation or poll taxes, and taxes on real estate.

---

[117] 3 Dallas, 171

[118] Springer v. United States, 102 U.S., 586.

There the matter rested until the year 1894 when Congress enacted another income tax law. This time the argument from necessity was lacking. The country was in a state of profound peace. Opposition to the tax among the moneyed interests was widespread. Test suits were brought and after most elaborate and exhaustive argument and reargument the Hylton and Springer cases were distinguished and the act was held unconstitutional.[119] The decision was by a closely divided Court (five to four), the majority finally holding that "direct taxes" within the meaning of the Constitution included taxes on personal property and the income of personal property, as well as taxes on real estate and the rents or income of real estate. This conclusion was fatal to the act. It was conceded that the tax, in so far as it affected income derived from a business or profession, was an indirect tax and therefore valid without apportionment among the states, but the provisions for taxing the income of real and personal property were held to be an essential part of the taxing scheme invalidating the whole statute.

This momentous decision was almost as unpopular with Congress and the general public as the decision in Chisholm v. Georgia had been a hundred years earlier. Many legislators were in favor of enacting another income tax law forthwith and endeavoring to coerce the Court, through the force of legislative and popular opinion, to overrule its decision. Calmer counsels prevailed, however, and plans were initiated to get over the difficulty by a constitutional amendment. Meanwhile, steps were taken to eke out the national revenue by various excise taxes, notably the so-called Federal Corporation Tax. This novel tax, which was thought by many to involve a very serious encroachment by the Federal Government on the powers of the states, will be discussed more at length in later chapters.[120]

The constitutional amendment as proposed by Congress and ratified by the states provided:

> *"The Congress shall have power to lay and collect taxes on incomes, from whatever source derived, without apportionment among the several states, and without regard to any census or enumeration."*

---

[119] Pollock v. Farmers Loan & Trust Co, 157 U.S., 429; same case on rehearing, 158 U.S., 601.

[120] See Chapters X and XI, infra.

Thus far we have dealt only with such limitations upon the federal taxing power as are expressly imposed by the Constitution. As has been seen, the only express limitations are that direct taxes shall be apportioned among the states, that indirect taxes shall be uniform, and that exports shall not be taxed at all. There are, however, certain other limitations which we proceed to notice briefly.

The Constitution provides[121] that the compensation of federal judges "shall not be diminished during their continuance in office." There is a similar provision as to the compensation of the President.[122] No attempt seems to have been made to tax the compensation of federal judges prior to 1862. A statute of that year subjected the salaries of all civil officers of the United States to an income tax and was construed by the revenue officers as including the compensation of the President and the judges. Chief Justice Taney, the head of the judiciary, wrote the Secretary of the Treasury a letter[123] protesting against the tax as a virtual diminution of judicial compensation in violation of the constitutional provision. No heed was paid to the protest at the time but some years later, upon the strength of an opinion by Attorney General Hoar, the tax on the compensation of the President and the judges was discontinued and the amounts theretofore collected were refunded. There the matter rested until after the Income Tax Amendment, when Congress again sought to impose a tax upon the income of the President and the judges. A federal judge of a Kentucky district contested the tax and the question came up before the Supreme Court for final decision. On behalf of the revenue department it was urged that a general income tax, operating alike on all classes, did not involve any violation of the constitutional provision. It was also contended that such a tax was expressly authorized by the Sixteenth Amendment giving Congress power to tax incomes "from whatever source derived." The Court in an exhaustive opinion[124] overruled both these contentions and held the tax to be a violation of the Constitution.

---

[121] Art. 3, Sec. 1.

[122] Art. 2, Sec. 1, Clause 6.

[123] See 157 U.S., 701.

[124] Evans v. Gore, 253 U.S., 245.

It has often been asserted that a limitation of the federal taxing power is found in the "due process" clause of the Fifth Amendment of the Constitution, providing that no person shall "be deprived of life, liberty, or property without due process of law." This amendment relates to the powers of the General Government. A similar limitation on the powers of the states is found in the Fourteenth Amendment. Taxing laws have frequently been attacked in the courts on the ground that, by reason of some inequality or injustice in their provisions, the taxpayer was deprived of his property without due process of law. In cases involving state laws such objections have sometimes been sustained.[125] There seems, however, to have been no case in which a federal taxing law was declared invalid on this ground, and the Supreme Court has recently remarked that it is "well settled that such clause (viz., the due process clause of the Fifth Amendment) is not a limitation upon the taxing power conferred upon Congress by the Constitution."[126] Nevertheless, it is believed that if a federal tax were clearly imposed for other than a public use, or were imposed on tangible property lying outside the national jurisdiction, or were so arbitrary and without basis for classification as to amount to confiscation, relief might be obtained under the due process clause of the Fifth Amendment.

By far the most important and interesting of the implied limitations of the federal taxing power remains to be noticed. That is the limitation which prohibits the National Government from burdening by taxation the property or revenues or obligations of a state, or the emoluments of a state official, or anything connected with the exercise by a state of one of its governmental functions. In other words, while the National Government may tax income from bonds issued by England or France or their cities, it is powerless to tax the income from bonds of Rhode Island or the smallest of its towns. This implied limitation, nowhere categorically expressed but enunciated in a series of decisions of the Supreme Court, has not always met with acquiescence from the executive and legislative branches of the Government. In fact, Congress is now engaged in an effort to do away with it, at least in so far as concerns the right to tax the income from state and municipal bonds. Today, however, it still stands as one of the most striking

---

[125] See, e.g., Union Tank Line Co. v. Wright, 249 U.S., 275.

[126] Brushaber v. Union Pacific R.R, 240 U.S., 24.

and unique characteristics of our governmental system. It will be discussed more at length in the next chapter.

Chapter IX
CAN CONGRESS TAX THE INCOME FROM STATE AND MUNICIPAL BONDS?

That is a question which is agitating a good many people just now. Congress from time to time has seemed disposed to try it, in spite of misgivings as to the constitutionality of such legislation.[127] A recent Revenue Bill contained provisions taxing the income of future issues of such obligations, and a motion for the elimination of those provisions was defeated in the House 132 to 61. Meanwhile, protests were pouring in from state and municipal officers assailing the justice and expediency of such a tax.

It is not the purpose of this chapter to discuss the questions of justice and expediency (as to which there is much to be said on both sides) but rather to deal with the strictly legal aspects of the matter and indicate briefly why such a tax cannot be laid without a change in our fundamental law.

Let it be said at the outset that no express provision of the United States Constitution forbids. On the contrary, that instrument confers on Congress the power to lay taxes without any restriction or limitation save that exports shall not be taxed, that duties, imposts, and excises shall be uniform throughout the United States, and that direct taxes must be apportioned among the states in proportion to population. The obstacle lies rather in an implied limitation inherent in our dual system of government and formulated in decisions of the Supreme Court.

The founders of this republic established a form of government wherein the states, though subordinate to the Federal Government in all matters within its jurisdiction, nevertheless remained distinct bodies politic, each one supreme in its own sphere. In the famous phrase of Salmon P. Chase, pronouncing judgment as Chief Justice of the Supreme Court[128]:

---

[127] See, e.g., H. Report No. 767, 65th Cong., 2d Sess., accompanying House Revenue Bill of 1918 as reported by Mr. Kitchin from the Committee on Ways and Means, page 89.
[128] Texas v. White, 7 Wall., 700, 725.

"The Constitution in all its provisions looks to an indestructible Union, composed of indestructible states."

In a later case[129] another eminent justice (Samuel Nelson of New York) put the matter thus:

"The General Government, and the states, although both exist within the same territorial limits, are separate and distinct sovereignties, acting separately and independently of each other, within their respective spheres. The former, in its appropriate sphere, is supreme; but the states within the limits of their powers not granted, or, in the language of the 10th Amendment, "reserved", are as independent of the General Government as that government within its sphere is independent of the states."

It follows that the two governments, national and state, must each exercise its powers so as not to interfere with the free and full exercise by the other of its powers. To do otherwise would be contrary to the fundamental compact embodied in the Constitution--in other words, it would be "unconstitutional".

This proposition was affirmed at an early day by Chief Justice John Marshall in the great case of McCulloch vs. The State of Maryland[130], which involved the attempt of a state to tax the operations of a national bank. That case is one of the landmarks of American constitutional law. While it did not expressly decide that the Federal Government could not tax a state instrumentality but only the converse, i.e., that a state could not tax an instrumentality of the nation, the Court has held in many subsequent decisions that the proposition enunciated by the great Chief Justice works both ways. For example, it has declared that a state cannot tax the obligations of the United States because such a tax operates upon the power of the Federal Government to borrow money[131] and conversely, that

---

[129] The Collector v. Day, 11 Wall., 113, 124.

[130] 4 Wheaton, 316.

[131] Weston v. City of Charleston, 2 Pet., 449.

Congress cannot tax the obligations of a state for the same reason;[132] that a state cannot tax the emoluments of an official of the United States[133] and conversely, that the United States cannot tax the salary of a state official;[134] that a state cannot impose a tax on the property or revenues of the United States[135] and conversely, that Congress cannot tax the property or revenues of a state or a municipality thereof.[136]

The Supreme Court has said (and many times reiterated in substance) that the National Government *"cannot exercise its power of taxation so as to destroy the state governments, or embarrass their lawful action."*[137] One of the most distinguished writers on American Constitutional law (Thomas M. Cooley, Chief Justice of the Supreme Court of Michigan and afterward Chairman of the federal Interstate Commerce Commission) has said:

> *"There is nothing in the Constitution which can be made to admit of any interference by Congress with the secure existence of any state authority within its lawful bounds. And any such interference by the indirect means of taxation is quite as much beyond the power of the national legislature as if the interference were direct and extreme."*[138]

The question as to the right of Congress to levy an income tax on municipal securities came up squarely in the famous Income Tax Cases[139] involving the constitutionality of the Income Tax Law of 1804. While the Supreme Court was sharply divided as to the constitutionality of other features of the law, it was unanimous as to the lack of authority in the United States to tax the interest on municipal bonds.

The decision in those cases is the law to-day (except in so far as it has been changed by the recent Sixteenth Amendment) with one possible

---

[132] Mercantile Bank v. New York, 121 U.S., 138, 162.

[133] Dobbins v. Commissioner of Erie County, 16 Pet., 435.

[134] Collector v. Day, 11 Wall., 113.

[135] Van Brocklin v. Tennessee, 117 U.S., 151.

[136] United States v. Railroad Co., 17 Wall., 322.

[137] Railroad Co. v. Peniston, 18 Wall., 5, 30.

[138] Cooley's Constitutional Limitations, 7th Ed., 684.

[139] Pollock v. Farmers Loan & Trust Co., 157 U.S., 429; same case on rehearing, 158 U.S., 601.

limitation. It has been held that state agencies and instrumentalities, in order to be exempt from national taxation, must be of a strictly governmental character; the exemption does not extend to agencies and instrumentalities used by the state in carrying on an ordinary private business. This was decided in the South Carolina Dispensary case.[140] The State of South Carolina had taken over the business of selling liquor and the case involved a federal tax upon such business. The Court, while reaffirming the general doctrine, nevertheless upheld the tax on the ground that the business was not of a strictly governmental character. This decision suggests the possibility that if an attempt were made to tax state and municipal bonds the Court might draw a distinction based on the purpose for which the bonds were issued, and hold that only such as were issued for strictly governmental purposes were exempt.

It remains to consider the effect of the Sixteenth Amendment.

After the Supreme Court had held the Income Tax Law of 1894 unconstitutional on the ground that it was a direct tax and had not been apportioned among the states in proportion to population the Sixteenth Amendment to the Constitution was proposed and ratified. This amendment provides that:

"the Congress shall have power to lay and collect taxes on incomes, from whatever source derived, without apportionment among the several states, and without regard to any census or enumeration."

When the amendment was submitted to the states for approval some lawyers apprehended that the words "incomes from whatever source derived" might open the door to the taxation by the Government of income from state and municipal bonds. Charles E. Hughes, then Governor of New York, sent a special message to the Legislature opposing ratification of the amendment on this ground.

Other lawyers, notably Senator Elihu Root, took a different view of the scope of the amendment, holding that it would not enlarge the taxing power but merely remove the obstacle found by the Supreme Court to the

---

[140] South Carolina v. United States, 199 U.S., 437, decided in 1905.

Income Tax Law of 1894, i.e., the necessity of apportionment among the states in proportion to population. This latter view has now been confirmed by the Supreme Court. In a case involving a tax on income from exports the Court said:[141]

> "The Sixteenth Amendment ... does not extend the taxing power to new or excepted subjects, but merely removes all occasion, which otherwise might exist, for an apportionment among the states of taxes laid on income, whether it be derived from one source or another...."

In a case decided a little earlier[142] the Court, speaking through Chief Justice White, had said:

> "By the previous ruling (i.e., in Brushaber v. Union Pacific Railway Co., 240 U.S., 1) it was settled that the provisions of the Sixteenth Amendment conferred no new power of taxation.... "

From what has been said it will be evident that the doctrine of exemption of state and municipal bonds from federal taxation is firmly embedded in our law and has not been affected by the Sixteenth Amendment. Whether it is a doctrine suited to present-day conditions is a question outside the scope of this paper.

The fear of federal encroachment, so strong in the minds of the makers of our Constitution, has become little more than a tradition. To many it doubtless will seem that any rule of law which operates to prevent the nation, in the great exigency of war, from taxing a portion of the property of its citizens is pernicious and should be changed.

If this be the view of a sufficient number the change can and will be made. Lawyers think, however, that it will have to be done by the orderly method of constitutional amendment, not by passing taxing statutes which a reluctant Court will be obliged to declare unconstitutional.

---

[141] Peck v. Lowe, 247 U.S., 165.

[142] Stanton v. Baltic Mining Co., 240 U.S., 103, 112.

Just now the tide of popular sentiment is setting strongly toward such a change. It was advocated in a recent Presidential message.[143] The immunity enjoyed by state bond issues is coming to be regarded less as a safeguard of state rights than as a means whereby the rich escape federal income surtaxes. One is tempted to predict that the next formal amendment of the Constitution will deal with this subject. If so, another inroad will have been made by the General Government on the failing powers of the states.

---

[143] Message of President Harding to Congress, December 6, 1921.

Elihu Root

Elihu Root (February 15, 1845 – February 7, 1937) was an American lawyer and statesman and the 1912 recipient of the Nobel Peace Prize. He was the prototype of the 20th century "wise man", who shuttled between high-level government positions in Washington, D.C. and private-sector legal practice in New York City.

Root served as the United States Secretary of War 1899–1904 under William McKinley and Theodore Roosevelt. In 1905, President Roosevelt named Root to be the United States Secretary of State after the death of John Hay. In January 1909, Root was elected a U.S. Senator from New York, and served from March 4, 1909, to March 3, 1915. He was an active member of the Senate Committee on the Judiciary. He chose not to seek re-election in 1914.

Chapter X
IS THE FEDERAL CORPORATION TAX CONSTITUTIONAL?

The most noteworthy enactment of the sixty-first Congress from a legal point of view, to say nothing of its economic and political significance, was the Corporation Tax Act[144]. That Act, forming Sec.38 of the Tariff Law, provides:

> *"That every corporation ... organized for profit and having a capital stock represented by shares ... shall be subject to pay annually a special excise tax with respect to the carrying on or doing business by such corporation ... equivalent to one per centum upon the entire net income over and above five thousand dollars received by it from all sources, etc. "*

The act goes on to require the corporations to make periodical reports concerning their business and affairs, and confers on the Commissioner of Internal Revenue a visitorial power to examine and compel further returns.

The genesis of the act is interesting. The growing demand for more efficient regulation of the corporations, so pronounced during President Roosevelt's Administration, had foreshadowed such legislation. It remained, however, for President Taft to take the initiative and mould the shape which the legislation was to take.

In the course of the Senate debate on the new Tariff Act it had become apparent that an influential party in Congress, backed by strong sympathy outside, was bent upon passing a general income tax act. The previous Income Tax Law had been pronounced unconstitutional by the Supreme Court as violating the provision of the Constitution that all direct

---

[144] Since this chapter was first published in 1909 as an article in the Outlook magazine the specific question propounded in its title has been settled by the Supreme Court (Flint v. Stone Tracy Co., 220 U.S., 107). The paper is here reproduced, however, in the belief that its discussion of the principles of our dual system of Government is as pertinent now as it was before.

taxes must be apportioned among the states in proportion to population.[145] That decision, however, had been reached by a bare majority of five to four. It had overruled previous decisions and overturned doctrines that had been acquiesced in almost from the foundation of the Government. A strong party was in favor of enacting another income tax law and bringing the question again before the Court in the hope that the Court as then constituted might be induced to overrule or materially modify the doctrine of the Pollock case. The President and his advisers viewed such a proposal with disfavor. To their minds the proper way to establish the right of Congress to levy an income tax was by an amendment to the Constitution, not by an assault upon the Supreme Court. Accordingly on June 16, 1909, the President transmitted a message to Congress[146] recommending a constitutional amendment, and proposing, in order to meet the present need for more revenue, an excise tax on corporations. The proposal, coupled as it was with a suggestion that such an act might be made to serve for purposes of federal supervision and control as well as revenue, met with favor and was enacted into law.

President Taft, himself an eminent constitutional lawyer, in his message recommending the law expressed full confidence in its constitutionality. The same view was taken by able lawyers who surrounded him in the capacity of advisers. The act is understood to have been drafted by Mr. Wickersham, the Attorney General, and vouched for by Senator Elihu Root and others of scarcely less authority in the domain of constitutional law.

Against opinions from such sources one takes the field with diffidence. I venture, however, to outline briefly some reasons for doubting the constitutionality of the act.

At the outset it is essential to determine the exact nature of the tax. Obviously it is not a tax upon income "as income". If it were, it would be obnoxious to the decision in the Pollock case as imposing a direct tax without apportionment among the states. The language of the act, as well as the declarations of its sponsors, clearly indicate that it is intended, not as a direct tax on property, but as an excise tax on privilege. The phraseology of the act itself is--"A special excise tax with respect to the carrying on or doing

---

[145] Pollock vs. Farmers' Loan & Trust Co., 157 U.S., 429.
[146] Congressional Record, June 16, 1909, p. 3450

business by such corporation," etc. Undoubtedly Congress has power to impose an excise tax upon occupation or business. This was expressly decided, in the case of the businesses of refining petroleum and refining sugar, by the Spreckels case,[147] referred to in President Taft's message. The message says:

> "The decision of the Supreme Court in the case of Spreckels Sugar Refining Company against McClain (192 U.S., 397) seems clearly to establish the principle that such a tax as this is an excise tax upon privilege and not a direct tax on property, and is within the federal power without apportionment according to population. "

What, then, is the privilege with respect to which the tax is imposed? Is it, like the tax involved in the Spreckels case, the privilege of doing the various kinds of business (manufacturing, mercantile, and the rest) in which the corporations subject to the operation of the law are engaged? Obviously not. No kind or kinds of business are specified in the act. The tax falls not only on corporations doing every conceivable kind of business, but also on the corporation that does no specific business whatever--the corporation which, in the language of an eminent judge, is merely "an incorporated gentleman of leisure."[148]

Moreover, if the tax were merely upon the privilege of doing business, it would seem to be obnoxious to the cardinal principle of just taxation that taxes should be uniform. In other words, if the privilege of doing a business--say conducting a department store--were the thing taxed and the only thing taxed, the rule of uniformity would seem to require that a corporation and a copartnership conducting similar stores on opposite corners of the street should both be taxed. Nothing inconsistent with this view will be found in the Spreckels case. The party to that suit was, to be sure, a corporation, but the act under which the tax was imposed applied to individuals, firms, and corporations alike.

It must be concluded, therefore, that the tax is not upon the privilege of doing the businesses in which the various corporations in the land are

---

[147] Spreckels Sugar Refining Co. vs. McClain, 192 U.S., 397.

[148] Vann, J., in People ex rel. vs. Roberts, 154 N.Y., 1.

engaged, but is rather a _tax upon the privilege of doing business in a corporate capacity_, or, in other words, upon the exercise of the corporate franchise. That this is so appears very clearly from the message of President Taft. He says:

> "This is an excise tax upon the privilege of doing business as an artificial entity and of freedom from a general partnership liability enjoyed by those who own the stock."

Assuming, then, that this is the real nature of the tax, is it constitutional?

Unquestionably Congress may tax corporations organized under federal laws upon their franchises; any sovereignty may tax the creatures of its creation for the privilege of exercising their franchises; but how about corporations chartered by the states and doing purely an intrastate business? A state confers on John Doe and his associates the privilege or franchise of doing business in a corporate capacity. Can Congress impose a tax on the exercise of that privilege or franchise? The power to tax involves the power to destroy.[149] If Congress can impose a tax of one per cent., it can impose a tax of ten per cent. or fifty per cent., and thus impair or destroy altogether the value of corporate charters for business purposes. Does Congress possess such a power? The Constitution puts no express limitation on the right of Congress to levy excises except that they shall be "uniform throughout the United States." But there are certain implied limitations inherent in our dual system of government. The sovereignty and independence of the separate states within their spheres are as complete as are the sovereignty and independence of the General Government within its sphere.[150] Neither may interfere with or encroach upon the other.

The right to grant corporate charters for ordinary business purposes is an attribute of sovereignty belonging to the states, not to the General Government. The United States is a government of enumerated powers. The Constitution nowhere expressly confers upon Congress the right to grant corporate charters, and it is well settled that this right exists only in the

---

[149] McCulloch vs. Maryland, 4 Wheat., 316.

[150] The Collector vs. Day, 11 Wall., 113, 124.

limited class of cases where the granting of charters becomes incidental to some power expressly conferred on Congress, e.g., the power to establish a uniform currency, or the power to regulate interstate commerce. On the other hand, the right of the separate states to grant charters of incorporation is unquestionable. By the Tenth Amendment of the Constitution it is expressly provided:

> "The powers not delegated to the United States by the Constitution nor prohibited by it to the states are reserved to the states respectively or to the people." The Supreme Court long ago said: "A state may grant acts of incorporation for the attainment of those objects which are essential to the interests of society. **This power is incident to sovereignty.**"[151]

The power to grant the franchise of corporate capacity being therefore inherent in the sovereignty of the states, will not a tax imposed by Congress upon the exercise of the franchise constitute an interference with the power? If so the tax is unconstitutional.

The Supreme Court has repeatedly held, that the National Government "cannot exercise its power of taxation so as to destroy the state governments or embarrass their lawful action."[152] In the case of California vs. Central Pacific R.R. Co.[153] the question was whether franchises granted to the Central Pacific Railroad Company by the United States were legitimate subjects of taxation by the State of California. The Supreme Court, in language frequently quoted in subsequent cases, discusses the nature and origin of franchises, concluding that a franchise is "*a right, privilege, or power of public concern*" existing and exercised by legislative authority. After enumerating various kinds of franchises, the Court remarks: "*No persons can make themselves a body corporate and politic without legislative authority. Corporate capacity is a franchise.*"

The Court continues:

---

[151] Briscoe v. Bank of Kentucky, 11 Peters, 257, 317.

[152] Railroad Company v. Peniston, 18 Wall., 5, 30.

[153] 127 U.S., 1.

"In view of this description of the nature of a franchise, how can it be possible that a franchise granted by Congress can be subject to taxation by a state without the consent of Congress? Taxation is a burden and may be laid so heavily as to destroy the thing taxed or render it valueless. As Chief Justice Marshall said in McCulloch v. Maryland, "The power to tax involves the power to destroy."... It seems to us almost absurd to contend that a power given to a person or corporation by the United States may be subjected to taxation by a state. The power conferred emanates from and is a portion of the power of the government that confers it. To tax it is not only derogatory to the dignity but subversive of the powers of the government, and repugnant to its paramount sovereignty."

It is true that the Court was here discussing the right of a state to tax franchises granted by the United States, and not the converse of that question. The reasoning of the Court would seem, however, to apply with equal force to the right of the United States to tax a franchise granted by a state acting within the scope of its sovereign authority.

Patent rights and copyrights are special privileges or franchises granted by the sovereign or government, and under the United States Constitution the right to grant patents and copyrights is expressly conferred on Congress. It has been held repeatedly that patent rights and copyrights are not taxable by the states[154]. As said by the New York Court of Appeals in a case involving the power of the state to tax copyrights:[155]

"To concede a right to tax them would be to concede a power to impede or burden the operation of the laws enacted by Congress to carry into execution a power vested in the National Government by the Constitution. "

Apparently the same rule would be applicable were the granting of patent rights, like the granting of ordinary corporate franchises, a prerogative reserved under our system of government to the states instead of being

---

[154] People ex rel. Edison, &c., Co., v. Assessors, 156 N.Y., 417; People ex rel. v. Roberts, 159 N.Y., 70; In Re Sheffield, 64 Fed. Rep., 833; Commonwealth v. Westinghouse, &c., Co., 151 Pa., 265.
[155] 159 N.Y., p. 75.

expressly conferred on the United States. By parity of reasoning, the Federal Government in that case would have no power to tax them. It is familiar law, reiterated over and over again by the Supreme Court, that Congress cannot tax the means or instrumentalities employed by the states in exercising their powers and functions, any more than a state can tax the instrumentalities similarly employed by the General Government. Thus, it has been held that Congress cannot tax a municipal corporation (being a portion of the sovereign power of the state) upon its municipal revenues[156]; that Congress cannot impose a tax upon the salary of a judicial officer of a state[157]; that Congress cannot tax a bond given in pursuance of a state law to secure a liquor license.[158]

In the light of these decisions it is not apparent how Congress can tax the franchises of those state corporations (and they are many and important) which perform some public or quasi-public function. A state, to carry out its purposes of internal improvement, charters an intrastate railway or ferry company with power to charge tolls and exercise the right of eminent domain. Is not the grant of corporate existence and privileges to such a corporation one of the means or instrumentalities employed by the state for carrying out its legitimate functions, and is not a tax by the Federal Government upon the exercise by such a corporation of its corporate powers an interference with such means or instrumentalities?

In any discussion of the right of Congress to tax the agencies of or franchises granted by a state, the distinction must be borne in mind between a tax upon "property" acquired by means of the franchise from the state and a tax upon the exercise of the franchise itself. The former tax may be perfectly valid where the latter would be unconstitutional. Thus, the Supreme Court has upheld a tax by a state upon the real and personal property (as distinct from the franchises) of a railway company chartered by Congress for private gain, while conceding that the state could not tax the franchises, because to do so would be a direct obstruction to federal powers.[159]

---

[156] United States vs. Railroad Co., 17 Wall., 322.

[157] Collector v. Day, 11 Wall., 113.

[158] Ambrosini v. United States, 185 U.S., 1.

[159] Union Pacific Railroad Company vs. Peniston, 18 Wall, 5.

It remains to notice briefly one or two Supreme Court decisions which are relied upon by the sponsors of the new tax law. Reference has already been made to the decision in the Spreckels case[160] which upheld the validity of the tax imposed by the War Revenue Act of 1898 upon the gross receipts of corporations engaged in the businesses of refining petroleum and refining sugar. The Court held the tax to be an excise tax "in respect of the carrying on or doing the business of refining sugar," and such it obviously was. It was not a tax upon the privilege or franchise of doing business in a corporate capacity, like the tax now under debate. On the contrary, the act expressly applied to "every person, firm, corporation, or company carrying on or doing the business of refining sugar...." The case, therefore, has no bearing on the point we are discussing. Had the act applied only to corporations, a different question would have been involved.

The case of Veazie Bank vs. Fenno,[161] upholding the statute which taxed out of existence the circulation of the state banks, has frequently been cited as an authority sustaining the right of Congress to levy a tax upon a franchise or privilege granted by a state. It is true that in that case the eminent counsel for the bank (Messrs. Reverdy Johnson and Caleb Cushing) argued unsuccessfully "that the act imposing the tax impaired a franchise granted by the state, and that Congress had no power to pass any law which could do that;"[162] and that two justices dissented on that ground. The conclusive answer to this argument, was, however, that the power of the states to grant the particular right or privilege in question was subordinate to powers expressly conferred on Congress by the Constitution; that Congress was given power under the Constitution to provide a currency for the whole country, and the act in question was legislation appropriate to that end. The case does not hold that Congress has any general power to tax franchises or privileges granted by a state.

The scope of this chapter does not admit of further reference to the decisions. It is strongly urged, however, that none of them, rightly construed, will be found to sustain the right of the General Government to impose a tax

---

[160] Spreckels Sugar Refining Co. vs. McClain_. 192 U.S., 397.

[161] 8 Wall., 533.

[162] See 8 Wall., p. 535.

upon the exercise of franchises granted by a state in the exercise of its independent sovereignty, and that such a decision would mark a new departure in our jurisprudence.

In the debates in Congress over the bill many good lawyers appear to have assumed, somewhat too hastily, that the tax in question was an excise tax on business or occupation like that involved in the Spreckels case, and that the only constitutional question, therefore, was one of classification under the provision of the Constitution that excises shall be uniform throughout the United States. No less eminent a constitutional lawyer than Senator Bailey of Texas, in a colloquy with the junior Senator from New York, put the matter thus:[163]

> **Mr. Root:** *May I ask the Senator from Texas if I am right in inferring from the statement which he has just made that he does not seriously question the constitutional power of the Congress to impose this tax on corporations?*
>
> **Mr. Bailey:** *Mr. President, I answer the Senator frankly that I do not.... I think the rule was and is that Congress can levy any tax it pleases except an export tax. Of course a direct tax must be apportioned and an indirect tax must be uniform. But the uniformity rule simply requires that wherever the subject of taxation is found, the tax shall operate equally upon it.*
> *I believe that Congress can tax all red-headed men engaged in a given line of business if it pleases.... I have no doubt if the tax fell upon every red-headed man in Massachusetts the same as in Mississippi or Texas and all other states, the law imposing such a tax would be perfectly valid.*

The difficulty with this reasoning is that it overlooks the fact that the privilege of being red headed is not a franchise granted by a sovereign state. From the viewpoint of constitutional law it may well be that Congress can tax a privilege conferred by the gods where it would be powerless to tax a franchise granted by the Legislature of New Jersey.

---

[163] Congressional Record for July 6, 1909, pp. 4251 to 4252.

Chapter XI
THE CORPORATION TAX DECISION

The immediate consequences of the decision of the United States Supreme Court[164] affirming the constitutionality of the federal corporation tax are so slight that its profound significance is likely to be overlooked. Until it was merged with the general income tax the exaction was not burdensome and proved easy of collection. The thing upon which it fell--the privilege of doing business in a corporate capacity--is an abstraction which makes little appeal to the sympathies or the moral sense. The public, more concerned with present conditions than with the passing of a theory, is indifferent.

Thus it has sometimes been with the turning points in the affairs of nations. They came quietly and without observation, and it remained for the historians to mark the actual parting of the ways. The Supreme Court holds, and in its opinion reiterates many times, that the tax is upon the "privilege of doing business in a corporate capacity."

Right here is the crux of the matter. Corporate capacity is not a right granted by the National Government. It is something which Congress can neither give nor take away. In the division of powers which marked the creation of our dual government the power to confer corporate capacity was reserved to the states. The decision, therefore, comes to this: Congress can by taxation burden the exercise of a privilege which only a state can grant. And the power to tax, it must be remembered, involves the power to destroy. This seems a long step from the theory of the men who founded the Republic.

Nearly fifty years ago the Supreme Court stated the theory as follows:

> "The states are, and they must ever be, co-existent with the National Government. Neither may destroy the other. Hence the Federal Constitution must receive a practical construction.   Its

---

[164] Flint v. Stone Tracy Co., 220 U.S., 107

limitations and its implied prohibitions must not be extended so far as to destroy the necessary powers of the States, or prevent their efficient exercise.[165]

The court buttresses its decision by the argument *ex necessitate*--that to hold otherwise would open the way for men to withdraw their business activities from the reach of federal taxation and thus cripple the National Government. The Court says:

"The inquiry in this connection is: How far do the implied limitations upon the taxing power of the United States over objects which would otherwise be legitimate subjects of federal taxation, withdraw them from the reach of the Federal Government in raising revenue, because they are pursued under franchises which are the creation of the states?... Let it be supposed that a group of individuals, as partners, were carrying on a business upon which Congress concluded to lay an   excise tax. If it be true that the forming of a state corporation would defeat this purpose, by taking the necessary steps required by the state law to create a corporation and carrying on the business under rights granted by a state statute, the federal tax would become invalid and that source of national revenue be destroyed, except as to the business in the hands of individuals or partnerships. It cannot be supposed that it was intended that it should be within the power of individuals acting under state authority thus to impair and limit the exertion of authority which may be essential to national existence. "

This argument will not bear scrutiny. It apparently loses sight of the vital distinction between a tax on the mere doing of business and a tax on the privilege of doing that business in a corporate capacity. These are two very different things. The right of Congress to tax the doing of business was not disputed. It had been expressly upheld in the well-known case of Spreckels Sugar Refining Co. v. McClain[166], which involved a tax on the business of refining sugar, whether done by a corporation or by individuals. The tax

---

[165] Railroad Co. v. Peniston, 18 Wall., 5.

[166] 192 U.S., 397.

under consideration, however, goes further and fastens upon something new- something which in the case of individuals or partnerships has no existence at all--which comes into being only by the exercise of the sovereign power of a state. The opponents of the tax, far from attempting to narrow the existing field of federal taxation, were in fact resisting an encroachment by Congress on an entirely new field, created by, and theretofore reserved exclusively to, the separate states. It was conceded that Congress could tax a business when done by individuals and could tax the same business when done by a corporation. The inquiry was: Does the act of a state in clothing the individuals with corporate capacity create a new subject matter for taxation by the General Government? That was the real question before the Court, and the decision answers it in the affirmative.

Other illustrations of the same apparent confusion of thought are to be found in the opinion. For example, it is said (citing various cases involving a tax on business where the party taxed was a corporation):

" *We think it is the result of the cases heretofore decided in this Court, that such business activities, though exercised because of state-created franchises, are not beyond the taxing   power of the United States.* "

Here again the Court seems to lose sight of the distinction between a tax on "business activities" and a tax on the privilege of conducting such activities in a corporate capacity.

It is futile, however, to quarrel with the logic of the opinion. The question is closed and the Court, by affirming the judgments appealed from, has committed itself to the theory that the Federal Government may, by taxation, burden the exercise of a privilege which only a state can confer. With the expediency of that theory as applied to present-day political conditions we are not now concerned. The object of this chapter is to point out that the decision marks a distinct departure from the earlier doctrine that the two sovereignties, federal and state, are upon an equality within their respective spheres.

In view of the centralizing forces which are tending to transform these sovereign states into mere political subdivisions of a nation, the decision is of great significance. Moreover, in a very practical way it touches the right of each state under the compact evidenced by the Federal Constitution to manage its internal affairs free from compulsion or interference by the other states. To illustrate: In some parts of the country the anti-corporation feeling runs high. Many men if given their way would tax the larger corporations out of existence. Under this decision the way is open whenever a majority can be secured in Congress. An increase in the tax rate is all that would be necessary. Make the rate ten per cent, or twenty per cent, instead of one per cent, and the thing is accomplished.

New York may deem it good policy to encourage the carrying on of industry in a corporate form. Texas may take a different view and conclude that the solution of the trust problem lies in suppressing certain classes of corporations altogether. Under this decision it lies within the power of Texas and her associates if sufficiently numerous to impose their view on New York and make it impossible for her domestic industries to be carried on profitably in a corporate form. And yet the possibility of impressing the will of one state or group of states upon another state with respect to her internal affairs is the very thing which the founders of the republic sought most carefully to avoid. Had it been understood in 1787 that the grant of taxing powers to the General Government involved such a curtailment of state independence, few states, in all probability, would have been ready to ratify the Constitution.

William Howard Taft, 27th President of the United States

Flint v. Stone Tracy Co. 220 U.S. 107 (1911) was a United States Supreme Court case challenging the validity of an income tax on corporations. The court ruled that the privilege of operating in corporate form is valuable and justifies imposition of an income tax.

President William Howard Taft proposed a constitutional amendment to allow federal income taxes on individuals and an excise tax "upon the privilege of doing business as an artificial entity and of freedom from a general partnership liability enjoyed by those who own the stock" on June 16, 1909.[1] The Sixteenth Amendment to the United States Constitution establishing federal income taxes was enacted in 1913; and the Corporation Excise Tax Act, sometimes known as the Corporation Tax Act, was enacted on August 5, 1909 and taxed corporation income at 1%, with the first $5000 exempt.

Henry Campbell Black stated:"*The tax laid by the act of 1909 was specifically denominated a "special excise tax" and was declared to be imposed "with respect to the carrying on or doing doing business by such corporation." This was in reality an income tax very thinly disguised, and restricted to corporations. But the theoretical distinction between a tax on income and a tax on the privilege of doing business in a corporate capacity, as measured by income, afforded sufficient ground for the courts to hold that it was not a direct tax and therefore not in conflict with the constitution.*"

CHAPTER XII
THE FEDERAL GOVERNMENT AND THE TRUSTS

The curbing of monopolies and combinations in restraint of trade was no part of the functions of the Federal Government as planned by the framers of the Constitution. To their minds such matters, under the dual system of government which they were establishing, belonged to the states. The Constitution was designed to limit the National Government to functions absolutely needed for the national welfare. All other powers were "reserved to the states respectively or to the people."

As time went on, however, and industries expanded it was seen that the power of no single state was adequate to control concerns operating in many states at the same time. The need of action by the General Government became manifest. Power in Congress to legislate on the subject, albeit somewhat indirectly, was found in the Commerce Clause of the Constitution, and in the year 1890 the Sherman Anti-Trust Act was enacted.

Few statutes have aroused more discussion or been the subject of more perplexity and misunderstanding. President Taft's remark, made after the decisions of the Supreme Court in the Standard Oil and Tobacco Trust cases,[167] that "the business community now knows or ought to know where it stands," was received with incredulity approaching derision. Yet from a lawyer's point of view (and it must be borne in mind that the President was a lawyer and is now Chief Justice of the Court) the statement cannot be controverted. The decisions in the Standard Oil and Tobacco cases did in fact dispel whatever uncertainty remained as to what the Sherman Act means.

The Sherman Act[168] declares unlawful every contract, combination, or conspiracy in restraint of interstate trade, and every attempt to monopolize interstate trade. The legal uncertainties that have arisen in its enforcement have not been with respect to the meaning of the terms

---

[167] Standard Oil Co. v. United States, 221 U.S., 1. United States v. American Tobacco Co., Ibid., 106.

[168] "An Act to protect trade and commerce against unlawful restraints and monopolies," approved July 2, 1890.

"restraint of trade" and "monopoly," although the popular impression is to the contrary. In 1890, when the statute was passed, contracts in restraint of trade and monopolies were already unlawful at common law, and these terms, by a long series of decisions both here and in England, had been defined as definitely as the nature of the subject matter permitted. While incapable (like the term "fraud") of precise definition covering all forms which the ingenuity of man might devise, nevertheless their meaning and scope were well within the understanding of any man of reasonable intelligence. Whatever legal uncertainties have arisen have been chiefly owing to two questions: first, What is "interstate" trade within the meaning of the act? And second, did the act enlarge the common-law rule as to what restraints were unlawful?

The act was nearly shipwrecked at the outset on the first of these questions. In the famous Knight case,[169] the first case under the Sherman Act to reach the Supreme Court, it was held that the transactions by which the American Sugar Refining Company obtained control of the Philadelphia refineries and secured a virtual monopoly could not be reached under the act because they bore no direct relation to interstate commerce. The effect of this decision naturally was to cast doubt upon the efficacy of the statute and encourage the trust builders. Perhaps the case was rightly decided in view of the peculiar form in which the issues were presented by the pleadings. In the light of later decisions, however, it is safe to assert that the Court would now find little difficulty in applying the remedies provided by the Sherman Act to a similar state of facts, properly presented. While no prudent lawyer would care to attempt a comprehensive definition of what constitutes interstate commerce, it may at least be said that the tendency of the courts has been and is toward a constant broadening of the term to meet the facts of present-day business.

The other question--Did the Sherman Act change the common-law rule as to what restraints and monopolies are forbidden?--has been even more troublesome. The lawyers in Congress who framed the law believed that it did not. This is the testimony of Senator Hoar in his Autobiography, and as he was a member of the Senate Judiciary Committee which reported the act in its present form, and claims to have drawn it himself, his testimony

---

[169] : United States v. E.C. Knight Company, 156 U.S., 1.

is entitled to belief. The Supreme Court, however, in this particular went further than was expected. In the Trans-Missouri Freight Association case, [170] which reached the Supreme Court two years after the Knight case, that tribunal decided by a five-to-four majority that the words "_every_ contract ... in restraint of trade" extended the operation of the law beyond the technical common-law meaning of the terms employed so as in fact to include all contracts in restraint of interstate trade without exception or limitation. This theory was strongly combated by the minority of the court, speaking through Justice (afterwards Chief Justice) White, and was denounced by many eminent lawyers, notably the late James C. Carter, then leader of the New York Bar, who predicted that sooner or later it must be abandoned as untenable. Their protests were well founded. The theory, carried to its logical conclusion, would have prohibited a great variety of transactions theretofore deemed reasonable and proper, and would have brought large business to a standstill. As a matter of fact, it was never carried to its logical conclusion, and six years later it was expressly repudiated by Justice Brewer; one of the five, in the course of his concurring opinion in the Northern Securities case. [171] Justice Brewer said that while he believed the Trans-Missouri case had been rightly decided he also believed that in some respects the reasons given for the judgment could not be sustained.

> "Instead of holding that the Anti-Trust Act included all contracts, reasonable or unreasonable, in restraint of interstate trade, the ruling should have been that the contracts there presented were unreasonable restraints of interstate trade, and as such within the scope of the Act.... Whenever a departure from common-law rules and definitions is claimed, the purpose to make the departure should be clearly shown. Such a purpose does not appear and such a departure was not intended."

Nevertheless, the troublesome question remained, to plague lawyers and the community generally, until it was finally put at rest and the statute once more planted on the firm ground of common-law rule and definition by the decisions in the Standard Oil and Tobacco cases.

---

[170] United States v. Trans Missouri Association, 166 U.S., 290.

[171] Northern Securities Company v. United States, 193 U.S., 197.

What, then, is this common-law rule which President Taft found so clear? No one has discussed it more lucidly than did the youthful Circuit Judge Taft himself in delivering the opinion of the Circuit Court of Appeals in the Addyston Pipe & Steel Co. case,[172] an opinion in which his two associates on the bench, the late Justices Harlan and Lurton, concurred. The rule may be briefly stated as follows:

> *"Every contract or combination whose primary purpose and effect is to fix prices, limit production, or otherwise restrain trade is unlawful, provided the restraint be direct, material, and substantial."*

Where, however, the restraint of trade is not direct, but merely ancillary or collateral to some lawful contract or transaction, it is not unlawful, provided it is _reasonable_, that is to say, not broader than is required for the protection of the party in whose favor the restraint is imposed.

A familiar illustration is the sale of a business and its goodwill, accompanied by a covenant on the part of the vendor not to compete. Such a covenant is collateral to the sale, and if not broader than is reasonably required for the protection of the vendee it will be upheld, although a similar agreement, standing alone and not collateral to a sale or other lawful transaction, would be in direct restraint of trade and unlawful.

So much for the alleged uncertainty of the law. Candid men must agree with President Taft that in the light of the Supreme Court decisions it is reasonably clear what the Sherman Law means. But the fact that "the business community now knows or ought to know where it stands" with respect to the law does not greatly help the business situation. The real difficulty lies, not in the uncertainty of the law, but in the fact that the law does not fit actual present-day conditions. This is partly because many of the trusts were organized with full knowledge that they involved a violation of law but in the belief that the law could not or would not be effectively enforced. The realization that this belief was mistaken has thrown a good many people into a state of very genuine bewilderment, but it is an uncertainty, not as to what is firm ground, but as to how to get out of a bog,

---

[172] United States v. Addyston Pipe & Steel Co., 85 Fed. Rep., 271.

once having gotten in. For the most part, however, the general feeling of insecurity is due not so much to having knowingly overstepped the law, as to a change in economic conditions. The spirit of the time is one of cooeperation and combination. It is manifested in the churches and colleges as well as in the marketplace. In the industrial arena, the tendency has been intensified by the invention of new machines and the resulting aggregations of fixed capital in forms designed for particular uses and incapable of diversion into other channels. Such rules of the common or customary law as were the outgrowth of an era of mobile capital and free competition no longer fit the conditions under which we are living.

In a conflict between economic forces and legal enactment there can finally be but one outcome. The law must sooner or later adapt itself to life conditions. The real problem to-day is--how shall this adaptation be accomplished; how can statutes be framed which shall check abuses without falling under the wheels of social progress? Right here a swarm of half-informed theorizers are rushing in where trained economists fear to tread. It is difficult and dangerous ground, but there is at least one measure of legal reform--take away the right of one corporation to hold stock in another--which might be urged with confidence were it not for the existence of sundry oppressive and conflicting state laws.

The abolition by law of the holding-company device is no new suggestion. It was strongly urged years ago by the late Edward B. Whitney. It was the keystone of the famous "Seven Sisters" statutes,[173] enacted with loud acclaim in New Jersey at the behest of Governor Woodrow Wilson (but subsequently repealed and thrown into the discard). Such a measure would be more effective and far-reaching than the public supposes. Nearly all the so-called trusts have been organized and are being held together in whole or in part, by the holding-company device. In many cases this has been done merely as an innocent measure of convenience. The device, however, is a perversion of the corporate machine to uses not contemplated by its inventors and fraught with danger. It is too powerful a weapon in the hands of those alive to its possibilities, enabling a small group of men with a relatively insignificant investment of capital to control a country-wide industry. Take the simplest possible illustration: The industry of

---

[173] Laws of New Jersey of 1913, chaps. 13-19.

manufacturing a particular commodity is carried on by a number of corporations scattered throughout the country with an aggregate capitalization of, say, $10,000,000. A, B, and C form a holding company to acquire a bare majority of the stock of each corporation, say $5,100,000 in the aggregate. They dispose of 49 per cent. of the holding company's stock to the public, retaining a working majority. At one step they have secured absolute control of a $10,000,000 industry with an investment of little more than one-quarter of that amount, and by pursuing the same process further they can reduce the investment necessary for controlling the industry almost to the vanishing point.

It is needless to enlarge on the possible abuses of the holding-company device. They are coming to light more and more. The remedy, however, is not as simple as it seems at first blush. A summary abolition of the holding-company device would result in great injury and hardship to industry. In the present condition of the corporation laws of certain of the states, the right of large corporations to operate through local subsidiary corporations is a practical necessity. Otherwise they would be subjected to well-nigh intolerable exactions and interference. It has been the policy in some states in dealing with foreign corporations to attempt to impose, under the guise of fees for the privilege of doing business in the state, a tax on all their property and business wherever situated. Some of the attempts have been nullified by the Supreme Court as violative of the prohibition of the Fourteenth Amendment against taking property without due process of law, but these decisions have not wholly remedied the evil or checked the ingenuity of state legislators. In some jurisdictions great corporations seem to be regarded as fair game for which there is no closed season.

Right here the scheme of federal incorporation brought forward during President Taft's administration has many attractions to offer. It would do away with the principal excuse for the holding company device, and pave the way for its abolition. It should satisfy the general public because it would clothe the Government with enormously increased powers of regulation and control; it should be attractive to the corporations because it would afford relief from many of the intolerable restrictions, not always fair or intelligent, imposed by state legislatures. Under present conditions the right of a corporation of one state to do business in another (other than business of an interstate character) rests merely upon comity and may be granted or refused upon such terms as interest or prejudice may dictate. The right of a federal corporation to do business in the several states, on the other hand, rests upon the powers conferred on Congress by the Constitution and is not subject to the whims of state lawmakers. Such a corporation is not "foreign" in the states into which its activity extends and state laws aimed at foreign corporations will not hit it. Moreover a corporation with a federal charter can always take its controversies into the federal courts (except when Congress expressly forbids)[174]--a right of extreme practical value where anti-corporation feeling or local prejudice is strong.

The scheme of federal incorporation presents some constitutional questions. As pointed out in a previous chapter, the Constitution nowhere expressly confers on Congress the right to grant corporate charters. Under Chief Justice Marshall's doctrine of "Implied Powers," however, it has become well settled that Congress has implied power to charter a corporation whenever that is an appropriate means of exercising one of the powers expressly conferred, for example, the power to regulate interstate commerce. The most serious constitutional question appears to be whether Congress can authorize such a corporation to manufacture, the process of manufacturing not being an activity of an interstate character. In any event, the difficulty could be surmounted by a constitutional amendment. In these days of facile amendment such a thing seems quite within the range of possibility.

The scheme of federal incorporation is by no means new. In the Convention of 1787 which framed the Constitution, Mr. Madison advocated giving Congress the power to grant charters of incorporation. The proposition, however, did not find favor, Mr. King suggesting that it might foster the creation of mercantile monopolies.[175]

---

[174] The Act of Jan. 28, 1915, took away this right in the case of railroad companies incorporated under federal charter (38 Stat. 804).

[175] See Farrand, "Records of the Federal Convention," Vol. II, pp. 615-616, 620.

This objection would scarcely be urged to-day, when the country-wide operations of the so called "trusts" have given them a national character and made their control by federal power a practical necessity.

CHAPTER XIII
WHAT OF THE FUTURE?

In the preceding pages we have observed from various viewpoints the impressive phenomenon of federal encroachment upon state power. It must have become obvious to the most casual reader that the tide is running swiftly and has already carried far. Hamilton was mistaken when he predicted in the "Federalist"[176] that the National Government would never encroach upon the state authorities.

What then of the future? Is the Constitution hopelessly out of date? Are the states to be submerged and virtually obliterated in the drift toward centralization? No thoughtful patriot can view such a possibility without the gravest misgivings. The integrity of the states was a cardinal principle of our governmental scheme. Abandon that and we are adrift from the moorings which to the minds of statesmen of past generations constituted the safety of the republic.

No mere appeal to precedents and governmental theory will check the current. The Americans are a practical people, moving forward with conscious power toward the attainment of their aims, along the lines which seem to them most direct. They are more interested in results than in methods or theories. Experience has demonstrated that federal control often spells uniformity and efficiency where state control had meant divisions and weakness. They favor federal control because it gets results.

There is another aspect of the matter, however. The burden of federal bureaucracy is beginning to be felt by the average man. He is being regulated more and more, in his meats and drinks, his morals and the activities of his daily life, from Washington. If he will only stop and think he must realize that no one central authority can supervise the daily lives of a hundred million people, scattered over half a continent, without becoming top-heavy. He must realize, too, that, even if such a centralization of power and responsibility were humanly possible, our National Government is

---

[176] Federalist, Numbers XVII, XXXI.

unsuited for the task. The electorate is too numerous and heterogeneous; its interests and needs are too diverse. Shall the conduct of citizens of Mississippi be prescribed by vote of congressmen from New York, or supervised at the expense of New York taxpayers? Will an educational system suitable for Massachusetts necessarily fit the young of Georgia? Such suggestions carry their own answer. In the very nature of things there is bound to be a reaction against centralization sooner or later. The real question is whether it will come in time to save the present constitutional scheme.

The makers of the Constitution never intended that the people of one state should regulate, or pay for supervising, the conduct of citizens of another state. They made a division of governmental powers between nation and states along broad and obvious lines. To the Federal Government were entrusted matters of a strictly national character--foreign relations, interstate commerce, fiscal and monetary system, post office, patents and copyrights. Everything else was reserved, to the states or the people. Here was a scheme at once explicit and elastic. Explicit as to the nature of the functions to be performed by the National Government; elastic enough to permit the exercise of all other powers reasonably incidental to the powers expressly granted. The Constitution is not, and never was intended to be, a strait-jacket.

Proofs abound of the adequacy of the constitutional scheme to deal with changing conditions. For example, when the Constitution was adopted, railroads, the most powerful economic force in our present civilization, were unknown. Nevertheless, the Constitution contains adequate provision for dealing with the railroads. They are instruments of interstate commerce and may be controlled by the Federal Government under the express grant of power to regulate such commerce. Similar considerations apply in the case of those nationwide industrial combinations popularly known as "trusts." Their activities are largely in the field of interstate commerce and are subject to control as such by the Federal Government. Theoretically, only such activities of the railroads and trusts as are of an interstate character fall within the federal jurisdiction. Everything else lies within the jurisdiction of the states. However, a practical people will not long permit matters which are essentially single and entire in their nature (for example, railroad classifications and rates) to be split up merely for purposes of legal jurisdiction and control. In such matters, therefore, some measure of federal encroachment is inevitable in order that industry and progress shall not be hampered. The encroachment, however, is more apparent than real. The industries are national in scope, and all the activities of each are more or less interwoven and interdependent. Hence state regulation of the intrastate activities may sometimes be overruled as an interference with federal regulation of the interstate commerce. There is nothing in this which involves any real violation of the Constitution. It is merely an application of Marshall's doctrine of implied powers.

Social welfare legislation presents a very different problem. Some of the most dangerous assaults upon the Constitution to-day are being made in that field. The leaven of socialistic ideas is working. Representative government is becoming more paternalistic. Legislation dealing with conduct and social and economic conditions is being demanded by public sentiment in constantly increasing measure. Such legislation for the most part affects state police power and lies clearly outside the scope of the powers conferred by the Constitution on the National Government. Moreover, "the insulated chambers afforded by the several states" (to borrow a phrase of Justice Oliver Wendell Holmes) are ideal fields for social experiment. If an experiment succeeds, other states will follow suit. If it proves disastrous, the damage is localized. The nation as a whole remains unharmed. The sponsors for such legislation, however, are seldom content to deal with the states. Reform was ever impatient. The state method seems too slow, and the difficulty of securing uniformity too formidable. Moreover, it often happens that some states are indifferent to the reform proposed or even actively hostile. Accordingly, recourse is had to Congress, and Congress looks for a way to meet the popular demand. There being no direct way, and public sentiment being insistent, Congressmen find themselves under the painful necessity of circumventing the Constitution they have sworn to uphold. The desired legislation is enacted under the guise of an act to regulate commerce or raise revenue, and the task of upholding the Constitution is passed to the Supreme Court.

Such subterfuges, far from arousing public condemnation, are praised by the unthinking as far sighted statesmanship. It is popular nowadays to apply the term "forward-looking" to people who would make the National Government an agency for social-welfare work, and to characterize as "lacking in vision" anyone who interposes a constitutional principle in the path of a social reform. Friends of progress sometimes forget that the real forward-looking man is he who can see the pitfall ahead as well as the rainbow; the man of true vision is one whose view of the stars is steadied by keeping his feet firmly on the ground.

It cannot be reiterated too often that, under our political system, legislation in the nature of police regulation (except in so far as it affects commerce or foreign relations) is the province of the states, not of the National Government. This is not merely sound constitutional law; it is good sense as well. Regulations salutary for Scandinavian immigrants of the northwest may not fit the Creoles of Louisiana. In the long run the police power will be exercised most advantageously for all concerned by local authority.

The present tendency toward centralization cannot go on indefinitely. A point must be reached sooner or later when an over-centralized government becomes intolerable and breaks down of its own weight. As an eminent authority has put it: *"If we did not have states we should speedily have to create them."*[177] The states thus created, however, would not be the same. They would be mere governmental subdivisions, without the independence, the historic background, the traditions, or the sentiment of the present states. These influences, hitherto so potent in our national life, would have been lost.

In a memorable address delivered in the year 1906 before the Pennsylvania Society in New York, Elihu Root, then Secretary of State in President Roosevelt's Cabinet, discussed the encroachments of federal power and expressed the view that the only way in which the states could maintain their power and authority was by awakening to a realization of their own duties to the country at large. He said:

> *"The Governmental control which they (the people) deem just and necessary they will have. It may be that such control would better be exercised in particular instances by the governments of the states, but the people will have the control they need either from the states or*

---

[177] Address of Supreme Court Justice Charles E. Hughes before New York State Bar Association, January 14, 1916.

from the National Government; and if the states fail to furnish it in due measure, sooner or later constructions of the Constitution will be found to vest the power where it will be exercised--in the National Government. The true and only way to preserve state authority is to be found in the awakened conscience of the states, their broadened views and higher standard of responsibility to the general public; in effective legislation by the states, in conformity to the general moral sense of the country; and in the vigorous exercise for the general public good of that state authority which is to be preserved."

Those words, spoken fifteen years ago, were prophetic. Moreover, they are as true to-day as when they were uttered.

Will the people see these things in time? Americans with pride in their country's past and confidence in her future dare not say No. The awakening may be slow. Currents of popular will are not readily turned. It is hard to make the people think. But if leaders and teachers do their part American intelligence and prudence will assert themselves, and the slogan of an awakened public sentiment may yet be: "Back to the Constitution!"

APPENDIX

CONSTITUTION OF THE UNITED STATES OF AMERICA

WE THE PEOPLE of the United States, in Order to form a more perfect Union, establish Justice, insure domestic Tranquility, provide for the common defence, promote the general Welfare, and secure the Blessings of Liberty to ourselves and our Posterity, do ordain and establish this CONSTITUTION for the United States of America.

ARTICLE I.

SECTION 1
All legislative Powers herein granted shall be vested in a Congress of the United States, which shall consist of a Senate and House of Representatives.

SECTION 2
The House of Representatives shall be composed of Members chosen every second Year by the People of the several States, and the Electors in each State shall have the Qualifications requisite for Electors of the most numerous Branch of the State Legislature.

No Person shall be a Representative who shall not have attained to the Age of twenty-five Years, and been seven Years a Citizen of the United States, and who shall not, when elected, be an Inhabitant of that State in which he shall be chosen.

Representatives and direct Taxes shall be apportioned among the several States which may be included within this Union, according to their respective Numbers which shall be determined by adding to the whole Number of free Persons, including those bound to Service for a Term of Years, and excluding Indians not taxed, three-fifths of all other Persons. The actual Enumeration shall be made within three Years after the first Meeting of the Congress of the United States, and within every subsequent Term of ten Years, in such Manner as they shall by Law direct. The Number of Representatives shall not exceed one for every thirty Thousand, but each State shall have at Least one Representative; and until such enumeration shall be made, the State of New Hampshire shall be entitled to chuse three, Massachusetts eight, Rhode Island and Providence Plantations one, Connecticut five, New York six, New Jersey four, Pennsylvania eight, Delaware one, Maryland six, Virginia ten, North Carolina five, South Carolina five, and Georgia three.

When vacancies happen in the Representation from any State, the Executive Authority thereof shall issue Writs of Election to fill such Vacancies.

The House of Representatives shall chuse their Speaker and other Officers; and shall have the sole Power of Impeachment.

SECTION 3
The Senate of the United States shall be composed of two Senators from each State, chosen by the Legislature thereof, for six Years; and each Senator shall have one Vote.

Immediately after they shall be assembled in Consequence of the first Election, they shall be divided as equally as may be into three Classes. The Seats of the Senators of the first Class shall be vacated at the Expiration of the second Year, of the second Class at the Expiration of the fourth Year, and of the third Class at the Expiration of the sixth Year, so that one third may be chosen every second Year; and if Vacancies happen by Resignation, or otherwise, during the Recess of the Legislature of any State, the Executive thereof may make temporary Appointments until the next Meeting of the Legislature, which shall then fill such Vacancies.

No Person shall be a Senator who shall not have attained to the Age of thirty Years, and been nine Years a Citizen of the United States, and who shall not, when elected, be an Inhabitant of that State for which he shall be chosen.

The Vice President of the United States shall be President of the Senate, but shall have no Vote, unless they be equally divided.

The Senate shall chuse their other Officers, and also a President pro tempore, in the Absence of the Vice President, or when he shall exercise the Office of President of the United States.

The Senate shall have the sole Power to try all Impeachments. When sitting for that Purpose, they shall be on Oath or Affirmation. When the President of the United States is tried, the Chief Justice shall preside: And no Person shall be convicted without the Concurrence of two thirds of the Members present.

Judgment in Cases of Impeachment shall not extend further than to removal from Office, and disqualification to hold and enjoy any Office of honor, Trust or Profit under the United States: but the Party convicted shall nevertheless be liable and subject to Indictment, Trial, Judgment and Punishment, according to Law.

SECTION 4
The Times, Places and Manner of holding Elections for Senators and Representatives, shall be prescribed in each State by the Legislature thereof; but the Congress may at any time by Law make or alter such Regulations, except as to the Places of chusing Senators.

The Congress shall assemble at least once in every Year, and such Meeting shall be on the first Monday in December, unless they shall by Law appoint a different Day.

SECTION 5
Each House shall be the Judge of the Elections, Returns and Qualifications of its own Members, and a Majority of each shall constitute a Quorum to do Business; but a smaller Number may adjourn from day to day, and may be authorized to compel the Attendance of absent Members, in such Manner, and under such Penalties as each House may provide.

Each House may determine the Rules of its Proceedings, punish its Members for disorderly Behavior, and, with the Concurrence of two thirds, expel a Member.

Each House shall keep a Journal of its Proceedings, and from time to time publish the same, excepting such Parts as may in their Judgment require

Secrecy; and the Yeas and Nays of the Members of either House on any question shall, at the Desire of one fifth of those Present, be entered on the Journal.

Neither House, during the Session of Congress, shall, without the Consent of the other, adjourn for more than three days, nor to any other Place than that in which the two Houses shall be sitting.

SECTION 6
The Senators and Representatives shall receive a Compensation for their Services, to be ascertained by Law, and paid out of the Treasury of the United States. They shall in all Cases, except Treason, Felony and Breach of the Peace, be privileged from Arrest during their Attendance at the Session of their respective Houses, and in going to and returning from the same; and for any Speech or Debate in either House, they shall not be questioned in any other Place.

No Senator or Representative shall, during the Time for which he was elected, be appointed to any civil Office under the Authority of the United States, which shall have been created, or the Emoluments whereof shall have been encreased during such time; and no Person holding any Office under the United States, shall be a Member of either House during his Continuance in Office.

SECTION 7
All Bills for raising Revenue shall originate in the House of Representatives; but the Senate may propose or concur with Amendments as on other Bills.

Every Bill which shall have passed the House of Representatives and the Senate, shall, before it become a Law, be presented to the President of the United States; If he approve he shall sign it, but if not he shall return it, with his Objections to that House in which it shall have originated, who shall enter the Objections at large on their Journal, and proceed to reconsider it. If after such Reconsideration two thirds of that House shall agree to pass the Bill, it shall be sent, together with the Objections, to the other House, by which it shall likewise be reconsidered, and if approved by two thirds of that House, it shall become a Law. But in all such Cases the Votes of both Houses shall be determined by Yeas and Nays, and the Names of the Persons voting for and against the Bill shall be entered on the Journal of each House respectively. If any Bill shall not be returned by the President within ten Days (Sundays excepted) after it shall have been presented to him, the Same shall be a Law, in like Manner as if he had signed it, unless the Congress by their Adjournment prevent its Return, in which Case it shall not be a Law.

Every Order, Resolution, or Vote to which the Concurrence of the Senate and House of Representatives may be necessary (except on a question of Adjournment) shall be presented to the President of the United States; and before the Same shall take Effect, shall be approved by him, or being disapproved by him, shall be repassed by two thirds of the Senate and House of Representatives, according to the Rules and Limitations prescribed in the Case of a Bill.

SECTION 8
The Congress shall have Power To lay and collect Taxes, Duties, Imposts and Excises, to pay the Debts and provide for the common Defence and general Welfare of the United States; but all Duties, Imposts and Excises shall be uniform throughout the United States;

To borrow Money on the credit of the United States;

To regulate Commerce with foreign Nations, and among the several States, and with the Indian Tribes;

To establish an uniform Rule of Naturalization, and uniform Laws on the subject of Bankruptcies throughout the United States;

To coin Money, regulate the Value thereof, and of foreign Coin, and fix the Standard of Weights and Measures;

To provide for the Punishment of counterfeiting the Securities and current Coin of the United States;

To establish Post Offices and post Roads;

To promote the Progress of Science and useful Arts, by securing for limited Times to Authors and Inventors the exclusive Right to their respective Writings and Discoveries;

To constitute Tribunals inferior to the Supreme Court;

To define and punish Piracies and Felonies committed on the high Seas, and Offences against the Law of Nations;

To declare War, grant Letters of Marque and Reprisal, and make Rulesconcerning Captures on Land and Water;

To raise and support Armies, but no Appropriation of Money to that Useshall be for a longer Term than two Years;

To provide and maintain a Navy;

To make Rules for the Government and Regulation of the land and navalForces;

To provide for calling forth the Militia to execute the Laws of theUnion, suppress Insurrections and repel Invasions;

To provide for organizing, arming, and disciplining, the Militia, and for governing such Part of them as may be employed in the Service of the United States, reserving to the States respectively, the Appointment of the Officers, and the Authority of training the Militia according to the discipline prescribed by Congress;

To exercise exclusive Legislation in all Cases whatsoever, over such District (not exceeding ten Miles square) as may, by Cession of particular States, and the Acceptance of Congress, become the Seat of the Government of the United States, and to exercise like Authority over all Places purchased by the Consent of the Legislature of the State in which the Same shall be, for the Erection of Forts, Magazines, Arsenals, dock-Yards, and other needful Buildings;--And

To make all Laws which shall be necessary and proper for carrying into Execution the foregoing Powers, and all other Powers vested by this Constitution in the Government of the United States, or in any Department or Officer thereof.

SECTION 9

The Migration or Importation of such Persons as any of the States now existing shall think proper to admit, shall not be prohibited by the Congress prior to the Year one thousand eight hundred and eight, but a Tax or duty may be imposed on such Importation, not exceeding ten dollars for each Person.

The Privilege of the Writ of Habeas Corpus shall not be suspended, unless when in Cases of Rebellion or Invasion the public Safety may require it.

No Bill of Attainder or ex post facto Law shall be passed.

No Capitation, or other direct, tax shall be laid, unless in Proportion to the Census or Enumeration herein before directed to be taken.

No Tax or Duty shall be laid on Articles exported from any State.

No Preference shall be given by any Regulation of Commerce or Revenue to the Ports of one State over those of another: nor shall Vessels bound to, or from, one State, be obliged to enter, clear, or pay Duties in another.

No Money shall be drawn from the Treasury, but in Consequence of Appropriations made by Law; and a regular Statement and Account of the Receipts and Expenditures of all public Money shall be published from time to time.

No Title of Nobility shall be granted by the United States: And no Person holding any Office of Profit or Trust under them, shall, without the Consent of the Congress, accept of any present, Emolument, Office, or Title, of any kind whatever, from any King, Prince, or foreign State.

SECTION 10

No State shall enter into any Treaty, Alliance, or Confederation; grant Letters of Marque and Reprisal; coin Money; emit Bills of Credit; make any Thing but gold and silver Coin a Tender in Payment of Debts; pass any Bill of Attainder, ex post facto Law, or Law impairing the Obligation of Contracts, or grant any Title of Nobility.

No State shall, without the Consent of the Congress, lay any Imposts or Duties on Imports or Exports, except what may be absolutely necessary for executing its inspection Laws: and the net Produce of all Duties and Imposts, laid by any State on Imports or Exports, shall be for the Use of the Treasury of the United States; and all such Laws shall be subject to the Revision and Controul of the Congress.

No State shall, without the Consent of Congress, lay any Duty of Tonnage, keep Troops, or Ships of War in time of Peace, enter into any Agreement or Compact with another State, or with a foreign Power, or engage in War, unless actually invaded, or in such imminent Danger as will not admit of delay.

ARTICLE II

SECTION 1

The executive Power shall be vested in a President of the United States of America. He shall hold his Office during the Term of four Years, and, together with the Vice President, chosen for the same Term, be elected, as follows

Each State shall appoint, in such Manner as the Legislature thereof may direct, a Number of Electors, equal to the whole Number of Senators and Representatives to which the State may be entitled in the Congress: but no Senator or Representative, or Person holding an Office of Trust or Profit under the United States, shall be appointed an Elector.

The electors shall meet in their respective States, and vote by ballot for two Persons, of whom one at least shall not be an Inhabitant of the same State with themselves. And they shall make a List of all the Persons voted for, and of the Number of Votes for each; which List they shall sign and certify, and transmit sealed to the Seat of the Government of the United States, directed to the President of the Senate. The President of the Senate shall, in the Presence of the Senate and House of Representatives, open all the Certificates, and the Votes shall then be counted. The Person having the greatest Number of Votes shall be the President, if such Number be a Majority of the whole Number of Electors appointed; and if there be more than one who have such Majority, and have an equal Number of Votes, then the House of Representatives shall immediately chuse by Ballot one of them for President; and if no Person have a Majority, then from the five highest on the List the said House shall in like Manner chuse the President. But in chusing the President, the Votes shall be taken by States, the Representation from each State having one Vote; A quorum for this Purpose shall consist of a Member or Members from two thirds of the States, and a Majority of all the States shall be necessary to a Choice. In every Case, after the Choice of the President, the Person having the greatest Number of Votes of the Electors shall be the Vice President. But if there should remain two or more who have equal Votes, the Senate shall chuse from them by Ballot the Vice President.

The Congress may determine the Time of chusing the Electors, and the Day on which they shall give their Votes; which Day shall be the same throughout the United States.

No Person except a natural born Citizen, or a Citizen of the United States, at the time of the Adoption of this Constitution, shall be eligible to the Office of President; neither shall any Person be eligible to that Office who shall not have attained to the Age of thirty five Years, and been fourteen Years a Resident within the United States.

In Case of the Removal of the President from Office, or of his Death, Resignation, or Inability to discharge the Powers and Duties of the said Office, the same shall devolve on the Vice President, and the Congress may by Law provide for the Case of Removal, Death, Resignation, or Inability, both of the President and Vice President, declaring what Officer shall then act as President, and such Officer shall act accordingly, until the Disability be removed, or a President shall be elected.

The President shall, at stated Times, receive for his Services, a Compensation, which shall neither be encreased nor diminished during the Period for which he shall have been elected, and he shall not receive within that Period any other Emolument from the United States, or any of them.

Before he enter on the Execution of his Office, he shall take the following Oath or Affirmation:--"I do solemnly swear (or affirm) that I will faithfully execute the Office of President of the United States, and will to the best of my Ability, preserve, protect and defend the Constitution of the United States."

SECTION 2
The President shall be Commander in Chief of the Army and Navy of the United States, and of the Militia of the several States, when called into the actual Service of the United States; he may require the Opinion, in writing, of the principal Officer in each of the executive Departments, upon any Subject relating to the Duties of their respective Offices, and he shall have Power to grant Reprieves and Pardons for Offences against the United States, except in Cases of Impeachment.

He shall have Power, by and with the Advice and Consent of the Senate, to make Treaties, provided two thirds of the Senators present concur; and he shall nominate, and by and with the Advice and Consent of the Senate, shall appoint Ambassadors, other public Ministers and Consuls, Judges of the supreme Court, and all other Officers of the United States, whose Appointments are not herein otherwise provided for, and which shall be established by Law: but the Congress may by Law vest the Appointment of such inferior Officers, as they think proper, in the President alone, in the Courts of Law, or in the Heads of Departments.

The President shall have Power to fill up all Vacancies that may happen during the Recess of the Senate, by granting Commissions which shall expire at the End of their next Session.

SECTION 3
He shall from time to time give to the Congress Information of the State of the Union, and recommend to their Consideration such Measures as he shall judge necessary and expedient; he may, on extraordinary Occasions, convene both Houses, or either of them, and in Case of Disagreement between them, with Respect to the Time of Adjournment, he may adjourn them to such Time as he shall think proper; he shall receive Ambassadors and other public Ministers; he shall take Care that the Laws be faithfully executed, and shall Commission all the Officers of the United States.

SECTION 4
The President, Vice President and all civil Officers of the United States, shall be removed from Office on Impeachment for, and Conviction of, Treason, Bribery, or other high Crimes and Misdemeanors.

ARTICLE III

SECTION 1
The judicial Power of the United States shall be vested in one Supreme Court, and in such inferior Courts as the Congress may from time to time ordain and establish. The Judges, both of the supreme and inferior Courts, shall hold their Offices during good Behaviour, and shall, at stated Times, receive for their Services, a Compensation, which shall not be diminished during their Continuance in Office.

SECTION 2
The judicial Power shall extend to all Cases, in Law and Equity, arising under this Constitution, the Laws of the United States, and Treaties made, or which shall be made, under their Authority;--to all Cases affecting Ambassadors, other public Ministers and Consuls;--to all Cases of admiralty and maritime Jurisdiction;--to Controversies to which the United States shall be a Party;--to Controversies between two or more States;--between a State and Citizens of another State;--between Citizens of different States,--between Citizens of the same State claiming Lands under Grants of different States, and between a State, or the Citizens thereof, and foreign States, Citizens or Subjects.

In all Cases affecting Ambassadors, other public Ministers and Consuls, and those in which a State shall be Party, the Supreme Court shall have original Jurisdiction. In all the other Cases before mentioned, the Supreme Court shall have appellate Jurisdiction, both as to Law and Fact, with such Exceptions, and under such Regulations as the Congress shall make.

The Trial of all Crimes, except in Cases of Impeachment, shall be by Jury; and such Trial shall be held in the State where the said Crimes shall have been committed; but when not committed within any State, the Trial shall be at such Place or Places as the Congress may by Law have directed.

SECTION 3
Treason against the United States shall consist only in levying War against them, or in adhering to their Enemies, giving them Aid and Comfort. No Person shall be convicted of Treason unless on the Testimony of two Witnesses to the same overt Act, or on Confession in open Court.

The Congress shall have Power to declare the Punishment of Treason, but no Attainder of Treason shall work Corruption of Blood, or Forfeiture except during the Life of the Person attainted.

ARTICLE IV

SECTION 1
Full Faith and Credit shall be given in each State to the public Acts, Records, and judicial Proceedings of every other State. And the Congress may by general Laws prescribe the Manner in which such Acts, Records and Proceedings shall be proved, and the Effect thereof.

SECTION 2
The Citizens of each State shall be entitled to all Privileges and Immunities of Citizens in the several States.

A person charged in any State with Treason, Felony, or other Crime, who shall flee from Justice, and be found in another State, shall on Demand of the executive Authority of the State from which he fled, be delivered up, to be removed to the State having Jurisdiction of the Crime.

No Person held to Service or Labour in one State, under the Laws thereof, escaping into another, shall, in Consequence of any Law or Regulation therein, be discharged from such Service or Labour, but shall be delivered up on Claim of the Party to whom such Service or Labour may be due.

SECTION 3
New States may be admitted by the Congress into this Union; but no new State shall be formed or erected within the Jurisdiction of any other State; nor any State be formed by the Junction of two or more States, or Parts of States, without the Consent of the Legislatures of the States concerned as well as of the Congress.

The Congress shall have Power to dispose of and make all needful Rules and Regulations respecting the Territory or other Property belonging to the United States; and nothing in this Constitution shall be so construed as to Prejudice any Claims of the United States, or of any particular State.

SECTION 4

The United States shall guarantee to every State in this Union a Republican Form of Government, and shall protect each of them against Invasion; and on Application of the Legislature, or of the Executive (when the Legislature cannot be convened) against domestic Violence.

ARTICLE V

The Congress, whenever two thirds of both Houses shall deem it necessary, shall propose Amendments to this Constitution, or, on the Application of the Legislatures of two thirds of the several States, shall call a Convention for proposing Amendments, which, in either Case, shall be valid to all Intents and Purposes, as Part of this Constitution, when ratified by the Legislatures of three fourths of the several States, or by Conventions in three fourths thereof, as the one or the other Mode of Ratification may be proposed by the Congress; Provided that no Amendment which may be made prior to the Year One thousand eight hundred and eight shall in any Manner affect the first and fourth Clauses in the Ninth Section of the first Article; and that no State, without its Consent, shall be deprived of its equal Suffrage in the Senate.

ARTICLE VI

All Debts contracted and Engagements entered into, before the Adoption of this Constitution, shall be as valid against the United States under this Constitution, as under the Confederation.

This Constitution, and the Laws of the United States which shall be made in Pursuance thereof; and all Treaties made, or which shall be made, under the Authority of the United States, shall be the supreme Law of the Land; and the Judges in every State shall be bound thereby, any Thing in the Constitution or Laws of any State to the Contrary notwithstanding.

The Senators and Representatives before mentioned, and the Members of the several State Legislatures, and all executive and judicial Officers, both of the United States and of the several States, shall be bound by Oath or

Affirmation, to support this Constitution; but no religious Test shall ever be required as a Qualification to any Office or public Trust under the United States.

ARTICLE VII

The Ratification of the Conventions of nine States shall be sufficient for the Establishment of this Constitution between the States so ratifying the Same.

Done in Convention by the Unanimous Consent of the States present the Seventeenth Day of September in the Year of our Lord one thousand seven hundred and Eighty seven, and of the Independence of the United States of America the Twelfth IN WITNESS whereof We have hereunto subscribed our Names.

G'o: WASHINGTON----
Presidt. and deputy from Virginia

New Hampshire   { JOHN LANGDON
                { NICHOLAS GILMAN
Massachusetts { NATHANIEL GORHAM
              { RUFUS KING

Connecticut { WM. SAML. JOHNSON
            { ROGER SHERMAN

New York   ALEXANDER HAMILTON

              { WIL: LIVINGSTON
New Jersey { DAVID BREARLEY
            { WM. PATERSON
            { JONA: DAYTON

            { B. FRANKLIN
            { THOMAS MIFFLIN
            { ROBT. MORRIS
Pennsylvania { GEO. CLYMER
            { THOS. FITZSIMONS
            { JARED INGERSOLL
            { JAMES WILSON
            { GOUV MORRIS

           { GEO: READ
           { GUNNING BEDFORD Jr
Delaware { JOHN DICKINSON
           { RICHARD BASSETT
           { JACO: BROOM

           { JAMES McHENRY
Maryland
           { DAN OF ST THOS JENIFER
           { DANL. CARROLL

Virginia_ { JOHN BLAIR--
           { JAMES MADISON JR.

           { WM. BLOUNT
North Carolina { RICHD. DOBBS SPAIGHT
           { HU WILLIAMSON

           { J. RUTLEDGE
South Carolina { CHARLES COTESWORTH
PINCKNEY
           { CHARLES PINCKNEY
           { PIERCE BUTLER

Georgia { WILLIAM FEW
           { ABR. BALDWIN

Attest WILLIAM JACKSON Secretary

AMENDMENTS

ARTICLE I
Congress shall make no law respecting an establishment of religion, or prohibiting the free exercise thereof; or abridging the freedom of speech, or of the press; or the right of the people peaceably to assemble, and to petition the Government for a redress of grievances.

ARTICLE II
A well regulated Militia, being necessary to the security of a free State, the right of the people to keep and bear Arms, shall not be infringed.

ARTICLE III
No Soldier shall, in time of peace be quartered in any house, without the consent of the Owner, nor in time of war, but in a manner to be prescribed by law.

ARTICLE IV
The right of the people to be secure in their persons, houses, papers, and effects, against unreasonable searches and seizures, shall not be violated, and no Warrants shall issue, but upon probable cause, supported by Oath or affirmation, and particularly describing the place to be searched, and the persons or things to be seized.

ARTICLE V
No person shall be held to answer for a capital, or otherwise infamous crime, unless on a presentment or indictment of a Grand Jury, except in cases arising in the land or naval forces, or in the Militia, when in actual service in time of War or public danger; nor shall any person be subject for the same offence to be twice put in jeopardy of life or limb; nor shall be compelled in any Criminal Case to be a witness against himself, nor be deprived of life, liberty, or property, without due process of law; nor shall private property be taken for public use, without just compensation.

ARTICLE VI
In all criminal prosecutions, the accused shall enjoy the right to a speedy and public trial, by an impartial jury of the State and district wherein the crime

shall have been committed, which district shall have been previously ascertained by law, and to be informed of the nature and cause of the accusation; to be confronted with the witnesses against him; to have compulsory process for obtaining Witnesses in his favor, and to have the Assistance of Counsel for his defence.

ARTICLE VII
In suits at common law, where the value in controversy shall exceed twenty dollars, the right of trial by jury shall be preserved, and no fact tried by a jury shall be otherwise re-examined in any Court of the United States, than according to the rules of the common law.

ARTICLE VIII
Excessive bail shall not be required, nor excessive fines imposed, nor cruel and unusual punishments inflicted.

ARTICLE IX
The enumeration in the Constitution, of certain rights, shall not be construed to deny or disparage others retained by the people.

ARTICLE X
The powers not delegated to the United States by the Constitution, nor prohibited by it to the States, are reserved to the States respectively, or to the people.

ARTICLE XI
The Judicial power of the United States shall not be construed to extend to any suit in law or equity, commenced or prosecuted against one of the United States by Citizens of another State, or by Citizens or Subjects of any Foreign State.

ARTICLE XII
The Electors shall meet in their respective states, and vote by ballot for President and Vice-President, one of whom, at least, shall not be an inhabitant of the same state with themselves; they shall name in their ballots the person voted for as President, and in distinct ballots the person voted for as Vice President, and they shall make distinct lists of all persons voted for as President, and of all persons voted for as Vice-President, and of the number

of votes for each, which lists they shall sign and certify, and transmit sealed to the seat of the government of the United States, directed to the President of the Senate;--The President of the Senate shall, in the presence of the Senate and House of Representatives, open all the certificates and the votes shall then be counted;--The person having the greatest number of votes for President, shall be the President, if such number be a majority of the whole number of Electors appointed; and if no person have such majority, then from the persons having the highest numbers not exceeding three on the list of those voted for as President, the House of Representatives shall choose immediately, by ballot, the President. But in choosing the President, the votes shall be taken by states, the representation from each state having one vote; a quorum for this purpose shall consist of a member or members from two-thirds of the states, and a majority of all the states shall be necessary to a choice. And if the House of Representatives shall not choose a President whenever the right of choice shall devolve upon them, before the fourth day of March next following, then the Vice-President shall act as President, as in the case of the death or other constitutional disability of the President. The person having the greatest number of votes as Vice-President, shall be the Vice-President, if such number be a majority of the whole number of Electors appointed, and if no person have a majority, then from the two highest numbers on the list, the Senate shall choose the Vice-President; a quorum for the purpose shall consist of two-thirds of the whole number of Senators, and a majority of the whole number shall be necessary to a choice. But no person constitutionally ineligible to the office of President shall be eligible to that of Vice-President of the United States.

ARTICLE XIII

SECTION 1
Neither slavery nor involuntary servitude, except as a punishment for crime whereof the party shall have been duly convicted, shall exist within the United States, or any place subject to their jurisdiction.

SECTION 2
Congress shall have power to enforce this article by appropriate legislation.

ARTICLE XIV

SECTION 1
All persons born or naturalized in the United States, and subject to the jurisdiction thereof, are citizens of the United States and of the State wherein they reside. No State shall make or enforce any law which shall abridge the privileges or immunities of citizens of the United States; nor shall any State deprive any person of life, liberty, or property, without due process of law; nor deny to any person within its jurisdiction the equal protection of the laws.

SECTION 2
Representatives shall be apportioned among the several States according to their respective numbers, counting the whole number of persons in each State, excluding Indians not taxed. But when the right to vote at any election for the choice of electors for President and Vice-President of the United States, Representatives in Congress, the Executive and Judicial officers of a State, or the members of the Legislature thereof, is denied to any of the male inhabitants of such State, being twenty-one years of age, and citizens of the United States, or in any way abridged, except for participation in rebellion, or other crime, the basis of representation therein shall be reduced in the proportion which the number of such male citizens shall bear to the whole number of male citizens twenty-one years of age in such State.

SECTION 3
No person shall be a Senator or Representative in Congress, or elector of President and Vice-President, or hold any office, civil or military, under the United States, or under any State, who, having previously taken an oath, as a member of Congress, or as an officer of the United States, or as a member of any State legislature, or as an executive or judicial officer of any State, to support the Constitution of the United States, shall have engaged in insurrection or rebellion against the same, or given aid or comfort to the enemies thereof. But Congress may by a vote of two-thirds of each House, remove such disability.

SECTION 4

The validity of the public debt of the United States, authorized by law, including debts incurred for payment of pensions and bounties for services in suppressing insurrection or rebellion, shall not be questioned. But neither the United States nor any State shall assume or pay any debt or obligation incurred in aid of insurrection or rebellion against the United States, or any claim for the loss or emancipation of any slave; but all such debts, obligations and claims shall be held illegal and void.

SECTION 5

The Congress shall have power to enforce, by appropriate legislation, the provisions of this article.

ARTICLE XV

SECTION 1

The right of citizens of the United States to vote shall not be denied or abridged by the United States or by any State on account of race, color, or previous condition of servitude.

SECTION 2

The Congress shall have power to enforce this article by appropriate legislation.

ARTICLE XVI

The Congress shall have power to lay and collect taxes on incomes, from whatever source derived, without apportionment among the several States, and without regard to any census or enumeration.

ARTICLE XVII

The Senate of the United States shall be composed of two Senators from each State, elected by the people thereof, for six years; and each Senator shall have one vote. The electors in each State shall have the qualifications requisite for electors of the most numerous branch of the state legislatures.

When vacancies happen in the representation of any State in the Senate, the executive authority of such State shall issue writs of election to fill such vacancies: Provided, That the legislature of any State may empower the executive thereof to make temporary appointment until the people fill the vacancies by election as the legislature may direct.

This amendment shall not be so construed as to affect the election or term of any Senator chosen before it becomes valid as part of the Constitution.

ARTICLE XVIII

SECTION 1
After one year from the ratification of this article the manufacture, sale, or transportation of intoxicating liquors within, the importation thereof into, or the exportation thereof from the United States and all territory subject to the jurisdiction thereof for beverage purposes is hereby prohibited.

SECTION 2
The Congress and the several States shall have concurrent power to enforce this article by appropriate legislation.

SECTION 3
This article shall be inoperative unless it shall have been ratified as an amendment to the Constitution by the legislatures of the several States, as provided in the Constitution, within seven years from the date of the submission hereof to the States by the Congress.

ARTICLE XIX

The right of citizens of the United States to vote shall not be denied or abridged by the United States or by any State on account of sex. Congress shall have power to enforce this article by appropriate legislation.